MW00757940

25 DAYS, 26 WAYS

TO

MAKE

THIS YOUR

BEST CHRISTMAS

EVER

Other Books by Ace Collins

25 DAYS, 26 WAYS

TO
MAKE
THIS YOUR
BEST CHRISTMAS
EVER
ACE COLLINS

Z ZONDERVAN®

ZONDERVAN.com/
AUTHORTRACKER
follow your favorite authors

We want to hear from you. Please send your comments about this book to us in care of zreview@zondervan.com. Thank you.

ZONDERVAN

25 Days, 26 Ways to Make This Your Best Christmas Ever
Copyright © 2009 by Andrew Collins

This title is also available as a Zondervan ebook.
Visit www.zondervan.com/ebooks.

This title is also available in a Zondervan audio edition.
Visit www.zondervan.fm.

Requests for information should be addressed to:

Zondervan, *Grand Rapids, Michigan 49530*

Library of Congress Cataloging-in-Publication Data

Collins, Ace.
    25 days, 26 ways to make this your best Christmas ever / Ace Collins.
      p. cm.
    ISBN 978-0-310-29314-9 (hardcover, jacketed) 1. Christmas — Miscellanea. I.
Title.
BV45.C589 2009
242'.33 — dc22   2009015943

All Scripture quotations, unless otherwise indicated, are taken from the *Holy Bible, Today's New International Version™*. TNIV®. Copyright © 2001, 2005 by International Bible Society. Used by permission of Zondervan. All rights reserved.

Scripture quotations marked NKJV are taken from the New King James Version. Copyright © 1982, by Thomas Nelson, Inc. Used by permission. All rights reserved.

Scripture quotations marked KJV are from the King James Version of the Bible.

Any Internet addresses (websites, blogs, etc.) and telephone numbers printed in this book are offered as a resource. They are not intended in any way to be or imply an endorsement by Zondervan, nor does Zondervan vouch for the content of these sites and numbers for the life of this book.

All rights reserved. No part of this publication may be reproduced, stored in a retrieval system, or transmitted in any form or by any means — electronic, mechanical, photocopy, recording, or any other — except for brief quotations in printed reviews, without the prior permission of the publisher.

Interior design by Christine Orejuela-Winkelman

Printed in the United States of America

09 10 11 12 13 14 15 • 20 19 18 17 16 15 14 13 12 11 10 9 8 7 6 5 4 3 2 1

In memory of Lena Shell and Minnie Collins

CONTENTS

INTRODUCTION

A NEW, BRIGHTER VIEW

This book is designed to focus on the wonder and magic of the Christmas season. Christmas is about so much more than busyness and debt. Even in the midst of mad dashes to the mall, it's a season of light that can bring out the best in everyone who chooses to discover and follow the Light. By digging into the history of the holiday and sharing a few special stories, highlighting some deep and rich songs, and citing a handful of treasured Bible verses, I hope to give you a small portrait of the glorious picture that is Christmas.

If you tend to dread the holiday, I ask you to think about this: what would life be like without Christmas? If there were no Christmas, there would never have been a Christ. And the world would be a much darker place without all that goes into the Christmas holiday.

Thus, putting Jesus back into Christmas is essential in order for each of us to get the most out of this incredible holiday season. What may surprise you is how easy it is to see the reason for the season in almost every facet of the holiday.

I hope you enjoy this day-by-day literary Advent calendar. I pray that you find it a useful tool in squeezing extreme joy and awesome wonder out of the Christmas season. Most of all, I wish that what you read here will spiritually enhance the depth of your holiday experience. Christmas can be the most fulfilling and exciting time of the year. No one should miss the chance to enjoy every minute of the holiday experience.

Finally, how we celebrate Christmas will define how we respond to the New Year. The spirit of giving, forgiveness, and outreach we embrace during the holidays can establish a permanent pattern we can follow every day, year after year. How great would that be? When you find a way to keep the Christmas joy all year long, then, like George Bailey in the beloved holiday movie, you truly have a wonderful life. I hope this book sets you on that course.

Mighty Christmas,
Ace Collins

Day 1

Rediscovering Advent

Odds are that at this very moment you're surrounded or even bombarded by the sights and sounds of a modern Christmas. As early as the first week in November, some radio stations embraced an all-Christmas-song format that includes such "classics" as "Grandma Got Run Over by a Reindeer" and the Singing Dogs' version of "Jingle Bells." Newspaper flyers and television commercials have been alerting you to the "must buys" of the season. Add to all this the places you have to be—choir practices, committee meetings, food drives. And then there's the endless ringing of the bells. Driving across town, it seems Santa and his elves are everywhere.

Like a hungry monster in a 1950s horror film, Christmas seems to be stalking you, all the while looking for new ways to consume your time, energy, spirit, and money. No wonder many people get so overcome with the anxiety of the season that they try to hide from all things associated with Yuletide.

As we look to the next twenty-five days and think about how to get the most substance and joy out of the holidays, we'll explore ways to restore the real message of Christmas. We'll begin our exploration by taking a look at one of the season's earliest traditions, which began long before the arrival of commercialization. By knowing and embracing the original concept of Advent, we power through the modern craziness and find the true spiritual aspects of the holiday. We discover the spiritual depth that comes from knowing the real reason this all began.

For many, Advent is a foreign concept. They have heard of it and associate it with the Christmas season, but they don't know what it means. Even most Christians don't know the meaning of Advent or how it ties in to the holidays. This lack of understanding is not only true for those who don't attend church; it's true for millions who never miss Sunday services. Many denominations simply do not recognize this sacred Christian tradition. Others fail to explain Advent in ways that bring meaningful spiritual understanding to this custom. Yet to experience a rich and meaningful Christmas, it helps to understand and truly embrace Advent.

Let's take a look at why the meaning of Advent has been lost for so many. Before 1940 the retail holiday season was relatively short. Many people didn't even think about Christmas until around December 20. A great deal of the shopping and almost all the decorating were done on Christmas Eve. What transformed this time-honored week of Christmas into a full six-week holiday experience was World War II. With millions of Americans fighting the war in foreign lands that lay beyond two oceans, President Franklin D. Roosevelt asked folks to shop and mail their gifts early. To ensure that loved ones overseas received their packages by Christmas, these parcels were to be given to mailmen no later than the first week in December. Thus, in 1942 the Christmas rush began before Thanksgiving.

Four years later, after the war ended, the mold was cast. Christmas had grown into more than a month of sales, songs, and entertainment. It was great for stores and, on the surface, seemed enjoyable for most people. Yet lost in this merriment were time-honored church traditions. Buried the deepest was Advent. Now it's time to shine the spotlight on this tradition of Advent and embrace it as originally intended. If you're looking for a way to put the real reason (as well as a lot of joy) back into your holiday season, it's time to bone up on some powerful and meaningful historical Christian teachings.

Advent is a Latin word meaning "the coming." The Christmas tie-in to Advent dates back to the sixth century, when church leaders dedicated a special time to properly focus men, women, and children on the real meaning of

Christ's birth *and* life. This was a part of the holiday that was supposed to be packed with great spiritual revelation, a road map people were to follow all the way to the manger. During the Dark Ages, millions treasured the joy found in Advent. In our modern commercial world, with all of its distractions, this kind of contemplation would seem to be more important than ever. Hence, the information age is the perfect time to go back to the roots of Advent.

In the beginning, Advent started on the Sunday closest to November 30 and ran until Christmas Eve. Essentially, the church leaders of the day set aside four weeks to consider what the coming of Jesus meant not only to the world but also to every individual's soul. Though it was promoted by the church, Advent was meant to be a time of personal retrospect and growth for each believer. So if you've found yourself complaining that the real meaning of the season has been lost in the noise of jingling cash registers, it's time to take a second look at the quiet peace found in experiencing a real Advent.

More than fourteen hundred years after the first Advent season, many families use the symbols of Advent, but most do not grasp the full meaning behind these symbols. While lighting candles and opening calendars can be wonderful traditions, few pause to reflect on their faith, because most don't know the real reason for Advent. Knowing what Advent is changes everything. Consider the following three reasons for Advent.

1. Reflect on what it means for God to come to earth in human form as a baby. We see the baby Jesus everywhere during this time of year, but do we think of God when we think about that infant? Even at Christmas, many never stop to consider the miracle of God loving his children so deeply that he placed himself in a body like ours. This unawareness can change if, like the early Christians, we start our first day of December by considering this miracle birth and what it means to our lives.

Consider this fact: no one has ever changed the world in such a lasting way as did Jesus. Reflecting on how different everything is because of his life and teachings should make anyone want to honor his birthday. After you have meditated on the historic impact of Christ for a few moments, add his divinity to the equation. Billons of children have been born, but there has never been another like this one child. That alone gives you a new and fuller perspective of the holiday and is a powerful reason to celebrate Christmas.

2. Consider how accepting Jesus as Savior changed your very existence. For just a few minutes, think beyond Jesus' birth and consider his life. Think about what he said and did. Consider the power and influence of Jesus' life on your actions, your thinking, and your faith. When you realize that because of a child born in a manger, you have experienced a dramatic life change—you act differently, are more compassionate —you should then want to fully enjoy this year's holiday season. Just thinking about Christ's life should motivate you to want to put his teachings into practice as a way of celebrating the day of his birth.

3. Know that Jesus is coming back. While the second coming used to be an important facet of each Christian holiday, it is no longer a part of Advent. That's why it's important to consider what Jesus would think if he spent some time with you during this holiday season. Would he see your excitement in the way you greet others? As he observes you preparing for the special day, would he recognize your faith in the way you reach out to others? Would he see you living out his commandants to reach out to the least of these? Jesus is coming back, but we don't know when that will happen. So what we need to keep in mind is this: if he were to return today, would he see himself in us this Christmas?

If you live each day of the holiday season carrying the spirit of Jesus in your heart and reflecting his compassion, your days will be truly joyful from now through Christmas and well beyond. By embracing this living concept, you lift up others with your smile, your energy, and your joy.

One of the holiday's most beloved carols is "The First Noel." This song reminds us to look back at the beginning of the Christmas holiday and focus on what that first Christmas means to us and to the world. *Noel* can be translated as a loud and triumphal greeting that trumpets our great joy and faith. Thus, each moment of Advent, each day of it, is a time to remind ourselves what a miraculous thing happened when the babe was born in Bethlehem. And we need to remember that it happened not just to Mary and Joseph, a few wise men, and some shepherds; it happened to us too.

Right now, with your lengthy "to do" list, you might feel as though Christmas is too much to handle. But if you will focus on the three original lessons found in the historical Advent, you will not only successfully navigate the next few weeks but also enjoy them as you never have before. Advent, in its original form, remains a strong foundation for engaging the spiritual aspects of the holiday. It's the perfect way for you to begin to experience the full joy of the Christmas season.

~~~~~~~~~~~~~~~~

A Shortcut to the Spirit of the Season

The gospel of Luke has twenty-four chapters. Read one chapter a day during December, using this book as a biblical Advent calendar that puts your focus on the birth, life, and promise of Christ.

DAY 2

SHOPPING OFF THE LIST

Shopping—isn't that what this season is all about? It seems that everyone is urging you to buy, buy, buy. Retailers are begging you to bring your cash, your checkbook, your credit cards and fill up a cart. If you resist, they can make you feel as if you are nothing more than a reincarnation of Scrooge. Add to that the pressure of purchasing just the right present, and giving becomes a chore. The real joy of giving is lost. The true spirit of the season is all but forgotten. Your thoughts change from "Merry Christmas" to "Bah, humbug!" Is it any wonder that most folks burn out long before they wrap the first gift?

To get the most out of this Christmas season, view shopping in a new perspective: not as a duty but as a blessing.

You also need to take a second look at your list and add a few names that have never been on it before. How do you do this? Where do you start?

With so many voices encouraging us to shop till we drop, it's important to first open one of the Advent calendar doors to highlight Jesus' thoughts on giving. Jesus focused on those whose needs were such that any gift they received would be embraced and treasured.

> The King will say to those on his right,… "I was hungry and you gave me something to eat, I was thirsty and you gave me something to drink, I was a stranger and you invited me in, I needed clothes and you clothed me, I was sick and you looked after me, I was in prison and you came to visit me."
>
> Then the righteous will answer him, "Lord, when did we see you hungry and feed you, or thirsty and give you something to drink? When did we see you a stranger and invite you in, or needing clothes and clothe you? When did we see you sick or in prison and go to visit you?"
>
> The King will reply, "Truly I tell you, whatever you did for one of the least of these brothers and sisters of mine, you did for me."
>
> Matthew 25:34–40

As you begin the buying season, allow Christ's words to give your shopping a new perspective. Before buying for your family, buy for someone in great need. Don't do it by yourself; get the kids, the grandkids, and your friends involved.

Almost fifty years ago country music legend Willie Nelson was literally starving to death in Nashville, Tennessee. He was broke. One cold December afternoon, as the singer-songwriter wandered the streets of Music City, he noticed the merriment, the joy, and the excitement of the Christmas season. Nelson noticed something else too: a homeless man who had even less than he did. Both horrified and inspired, Willie went home and wrote a song called "Pretty Paper." In 1963 Nelson's socially inspired number became a big holiday hit for Roy Orbison. It has remained one of the season's most beloved songs. The melody Willie composed is so bright and cheery, most who hear it don't really listen to the words. If they did, they would learn the story of a man who really was "the least of these." And like most of the world's poor, he was forgotten and overlooked. Listen closely to this song. You will come to know a person who noticed and who asked about that needy person:

Should I stop,
Better not,
Much too busy.

Not many Christmases ago I was given the name of a woman in our community who didn't have enough money to buy gifts for her children. Armed with the names and ages of the kids, my wife and I went to the mall. The trip was not only uplifting; it was challenging. What do you buy for kids whose mother probably can't afford batteries and who don't have a DVD player? Because the purchases required thought, they took on more meaning. This was no rushed experience; each new purchase was made with extreme care. We were even able to challenge our children to become involved, by asking them to put themselves in the position of the kids from that family. What would they want if they had nothing? What would be important to them? Thus, our boys helped in the choices as our family was completely caught up in the spirit of giving.

Armed with several sacks filled with gifts, we raced home to begin wrapping these treasures. Because they had become so important to us, because we had so much of ourselves invested in them, we made sure each present was perfectly covered with the brightest, most beautiful paper we could find. After the ribbons were tied and the name tags attached, we drove to the other side of town to meet the family.

As we walked into their drafty home, several things hit me. The first was just how little this mother and her three children had. There was hardly any furniture. The beds were nothing more than mattresses on the floor. Only one room in the entire home was heated. The kids were wearing hand-me-down clothing, and the mom was dressed in a sweater she must have gotten a dozen years before. Yet their smiles, as they saw the sacks of gifts, lit up the room like a searchlight.

Suddenly the chill was replaced with warmth created by anticipation, joy, and obvious gratitude. They had given up on Christmas, and it had come anyway. Their prayers had been answered.

I watched the children carefully tear into their packages. I heard their laughter and saw eyes that reflected the happiness in their hearts. I wanted to hold on to the moment forever. I wanted to embrace it and share it with others, for I had experienced the true joy of giving. This was what Christmas was all about. This made it meaningful.

But all too soon it was over. As we got up to leave, the three-year-old girl grabbed my hand and asked if I would see their Christmas tree. I could hear the excitement in her voice and knew she was awfully proud of this symbol of holiday cheer. I gladly followed her into a chilly bedroom. There, tacked to the wall, was a single string of green lights. She laughed and giggled, thrilled at how beautiful her "tree" was. A dozen lights were all she had, and yet she saw them as the most magnificent tree in the world. My eyes clouded with tears. Her simple and joyful vision of Christmas put mine to shame.

The next time you see a sidewalk Santa ringing his bell, think about those who are receiving the gifts bought with that money. While it's good to toss a coin into the pot, that's only a starting point.

To maintain the true spirit of Christmas and experience the joy of the season, put the name of someone who is not on anyone else's list at the top of your list. Churches and local governments have lists of those who have fallen on hard times. Contact the Salvation Army or the Red Cross. One or two calls can get you the name of a family in need of help this year. Get your whole family involved. Show the real meaning of giving by not just buying gifts and wrapping them but delivering them too. Together. Then those you love will come to understand the real impact of Christ's primary directive found in Matthew 25.

You have the time to do something. You have the time to get others involved with you. Shelters for the homeless, children's homes, and food kitchens are always in need. Schools know which families need food and clothing. Senior citizens may be facing a lonely Christmas because their families won't be coming home for the holiday. These older folks may not have physical needs, but the gift of a visit or a plate of homemade cookies is a way to bring Matthew 25 to life. By doing for others, you follow in the footsteps of the one whose spirit is still very much alive.

More than a thousand years ago, the son of Duke Borivoy of Bohemia became the leader of his country. He assumed the crown when he was just fifteen years old. Raised by a devoted Christian mother, King Wenceslas had traces of the wisdom of Solomon, combined with the compassion of Christ.

To fully understand his subjects, King Wenceslas walked the streets of his nation and visited the people. He asked them about their problems and needs. He used their ideas to create a more open and friendly government. In a revolutionary move, he reformed his government and reshaped the nation to be built on justice and mercy. He reduced taxes and improved public services. Harsh laws common in the Dark Ages were tossed out as he created new edicts that brought light to a hopeless world. Yet that was only the beginning.

When he came upon abject poverty, King Wenceslas would send his pages back to his castle to get food and clothing. As he gave away much of his wealth, he explained that he was just following the example of his own King, Jesus. In large part due to King Wenceslas's generosity and kindness, thousands of pagan peasants turned to Christianity. It was a revival unlike any ever seen in the country.

Centuries before gift-giving became a part of the holiday tradition, the young leader embraced Christmas like no one ever had. Each Christmas Eve, he left his castle seeking out the neediest in his kingdom. Though often faced with terrible cold and blizzards, King Wenceslas never missed his rounds. With his pages at his side, Wenceslas delivered food, firewood, and clothing. After greeting all in a household, he would pray with the group and move on to the next home.

To fully enjoy this holiday season, embrace the joy not just of giving but also of giving to those whose needs are great. By following in the footsteps of a king who helped inspire the fictional Santa, by embracing Christ's words in Matthew 25, by seeking a Christmas beyond the pretty paper and elaborate decorations, and by opening your eyes to the plight of those around you, you will feel the real meaning of the season in your soul, and your shopping experience will be one you will never forget.

~~~~~~~~~~~

A Shortcut to the Spirit of the Season

Finding those in need is easy. Local malls and churches have an Angel Tree. The Marines always collect gifts for needy children through their Toys for Tots program.

MAKING CHRISTMAS MIGHTY

When I was a child, the much beloved Christmas carol "God Rest Ye Merry Gentlemen" confused me. In my early years, I even thought it was a plot created by parents to get children to go to bed earlier. If you think about the words, you wonder, "Why would God want happy people to go to sleep?" As a youngster, I believed that God would want happy people to stay awake and share his glory into the wee hours of the morning. In fact, I still feel that way today. If you carefully read each verse, the old carol really seems like a charge to get involved with sharing the joy.

God rest ye merry, gentlemen
Let nothing you dismay

Remember, Christ, our Saviour
Was born on Christmas day
To save us all from Satan's power
When we were gone astray
O tidings of comfort and joy,
Comfort and joy
O tidings of comfort and joy.

Like many of our most revered carols, "God Rest Ye Merry Gentlemen" was written during the Middle Ages by an unknown peasant. Yet, as the words prove, he understood the full power of the Christmas season. The lyrics spell out why Christ was sent to earth, they share some of the lessons Jesus taught during his ministry, and they acknowledge the great gift given to us by Jesus' sacrifice and resurrection. It would seem that the song's author wanted folks to get so excited by this good news that sleep would be impossible. Just why did he ask us to rest?

A host of words, such as *surfing*, *gay*, and *hip*, now have new meanings. The same is true of many words we find in old songs. During ancient times the English meaning for the word *rest* went well beyond the meaning we attribute to it today. The word also meant "make" or "keep." Thus, when "God Rest Ye Merry Gentlemen" was written, the composer's charge was for listeners to let God *make* a change in their hearts and minds about the good news found in Christ's birth and life. Just knowing this change in meaning transforms the way we think about the song. Yet to grasp the writer's full intentions, we must look at another word commonly associated with the holidays.

In England they say, "Happy Christmas," but in the United States it seems Christmas can't exist without having *merry* in front of it. Yet if the writer of "God Rest Ye Merry Gentlemen" could be transported from his time to ours, he might be both amused and aghast at the way we use that word.

In Old English, the word *merry* could mean happy, but it was also often employed in place of the word *mighty*. Robin Hood's companions were known as his Merry Men, but that didn't mean this famous band of warriors was happy; they were powerful. That's why the king was afraid of them. When Great Britain was called "Merry Old England," it was the most powerful nation in the world. "Eat, drink, and be merry" really meant that well-fed troops would always be ready for battle. Thus, when taken in context, the new meaning of "God Rest Ye Merry Gentlemen" becomes "God keep you mighty, gentlemen."

The difference between a Christmas that is simply happy and one that is mighty is huge! Why settle for the former when you have a chance for the latter? With the old carol in mind, it's time for you to have not just a happy Christmas but a powerful one as well. Right now, today, embrace the real meaning of "God Rest Ye Merry Gentlemen" and put this old carol's message of the majesty of faith into action.

So many times I have heard folks say, "Our Christmas just wasn't any good this year." If Christmas is weak, it's because we have opted to make it weak. This is the moment to evict Scrooge from your heart and replace the old grumpy character with the spirit of Christ. How do you begin that transformation? The best way to start is by looking at the life of the individual profiled in "God Rest Ye Merry Gentlemen." Open your Bible, turn to Luke, and consider one of the great lessons found in the parable of the ruler and his servants. With these words, Christ is challenging us to make the gift of Christmas—as well as all our other gifts—a powerful tool of witness and testimony.

> A man of noble birth went to a distant country to have himself appointed king and then to return. So he called ten of his servants and gave them ten minas. "Put this money to work," he said, "until I come back."
>
> But his subjects hated him and sent a delegation after him to say, "We don't want this man to be our king."
>
> He was made king, however, and returned home. Then he sent for the servants to whom he had given the money, in order to find out what they had gained with it.
>
> The first one came and said, "Sir, your mina has earned ten more."
>
> "Well done, my good servant!" his master replied. "Because you have been trustworthy in a very small matter, take charge of ten cities."

The second came and said, "Sir, your mina has earned five more."

His master answered, "You take charge of five cities."

Then another servant came and said, "Sir, here is your mina; I have kept it laid away in a piece of cloth. I was afraid of you, because you are a hard man. You take out what you did not put in and reap what you did not sow."

His master replied, "I will judge you by your own words, you wicked servant! You knew, did you, that I am a hard man, taking out what I did not put in, and reaping what I did not sow? Why then didn't you put my money on deposit, so that when I came back, I could have collected it with interest?"

Then he said to those standing by, "Take his mina away from him and give it to the one who has ten minas."

"Sir," they said, "he already has ten!"

He replied, "I tell you that to everyone who has, more will be given, but as for those who have nothing, even what they have will be taken away."

Luke 19:12–26

All of us have been given many gifts. There is no better time to take inventory of those gifts than right now.

In Luke, what does Christ ask us to do with our gifts? We are to invest them. How do you invest joy? By letting others see joy in your actions.

One of the first songs you learned to sing as a child was

"This Little Light of Mine." I'm sure you remember the words. The light that is created by the joy of the season is also the message that runs through all the verses of "God Rest Ye Merry Gentlemen." The joy is found in the knowledge of not just Christ's birth but also his life. What is the best way to share it? Through your attitude.

If you put a smile on your heart this season, it will appear on your face as well. A smile is a powerful tool. A smile can lift more weight that any crane ever constructed. It can lift the weight of the world off someone's shoulders. Your smile can make all those around you feel better. Your smile can ignite the Christmas spirit. So vow to start each day by embracing the gift of joy and letting it power the light revealed in the expression on your face.

Another gift to embrace this year is the gift of life. A life lived well is one of the greatest testimonies you can give others. As one Christian hero, Francis of Assisi, is reported to have said, "Give a sermon every day and occasionally use words." If we live this Christmas season recognizing the power of the message of Christ, it will show in every facet of our lives. People will notice. When you fully embrace the mighty message of the season, that light you set aglow with your joy will become a blazing beacon. Your life will become a blessing to others.

Greet people with a joyful "Merry Christmas" or "Mighty Christmas." Let the words spring from your lips like an exuberant melody. Reveal by the happy look on your face and the enthusiasm in your tone that you are filled with the season's spirit. By doing this simple act, your life will become a sermon so needed by others at Christmas.

Another gift to recognize during this time of year is the gift of peace. To fully appreciate this precious gift, let's look through the lens used by the writer of "God Rest Ye Merry Gentlemen."

The peasants in Old England didn't have an easy life. They worked long hours, had few physical rewards, had no upward mobility, and were part of a class system that allowed them little say in their government. Their dreams were held in check by the brutal fact of being born into a low station in life. If you were born a poor peasant, you were destined to stay a poor peasant. Yet despite knowing he probably would never have anything of great value, the composer of the old carol had a rock-solid peace in his life. You can see this in the words he gave us in his song.

Consider another great carol of the season: "Go Tell It on the Mountain." This song was written by an American slave. Its composer also found great peace in knowing that Christ had come for him. You can hear the power of that message in his lyrics. In spite of the lot he had been given in life, he had found personal peace and power, thanks to the gift of the Christmas season.

So can you bring peace to the whole earth? Probably not. Leaders have been trying to do that for thousands of years, with dismal results. But if you believe in the reason for the season, you can find peace in your own life. The best way to start this quest for personal peace is by ending the conflict in your own world. If a problem is upsetting you, use the holiday season to put that problem behind you. Find the person at the heart of the problem and build a bridge to peace. Humble yourself, end a feud, seek middle ground, and in the process take charge of your Christmas.

Finally, maybe the best gift we Christians have been given is that Christmas has become so secular. Unlike Easter, which is seen only as a Christian holiday, this season has a universal nature that gives us a chance to take to a new level Christ's challenge of investing our gifts. The secularism of the season has given us many opportunities to tell the story found in "God Rest Ye Merry Gentlemen." Because Christmas is so universal, it is easier to talk about Jesus at Christmastime than to do so at any other time of the year. We need to invest this treasure we have been given and see it multiply.

Now is the moment to embrace the gifts we have been given as Christians. We have the power to make this a mighty Christmas, but to do that we must invest our gifts.

~~~~~~~~

A Shortcut to the Spirit of the Season

Use an old oil lamp as a part of this year's decorations. Fill the lamp with scented oil and light it each day as a reminder of your potential to be a light in a dark world.

SINGING A CAROL OF HOPE

This is the season when songs are literally in the air. You hear Christmas carols on the radio, in elevators, at church, on street corners, via the web, and in TV commercials. No matter where you turn, you simply cannot avoid the music of the season. Yet for many, Christmas music is just background noise. They are aware a song is playing but never listen to the words.

The message embraced by a majority of holiday lyrics, both sacred and secular, is upbeat and optimistic. As we listen, these songs lift us up and make us feel good. How can one hear "Jingle Bells" or "The Chipmunk Song" and not smile? Consider the hope and warmth found in such secular songs as "Silver Bells" and "The Christmas Song" ("Chest-

nuts roasting on an open fire ..."). Even beyond the traditional Christian carols, the spirit of the season is alive in
music. Listening to that message, we find our spirits buoyed
during even the worst of times. In fact, the meaning found
in two popular Yuletide offerings, "If Every Day Was Like
Christmas" and "We Need a Little Christmas," fully echoes
the joy and hope found in this special season. But if you don't
listen to the lyrics, you might just miss that point altogether.
So don't dismiss "White Christmas" or "Let It Snow" as el-
evator music. Instead revel in their simple but compelling
messages.

Probably no sermon has ever touched souls in as pas-
sionate a way as have "O Little Town of Bethlehem," "Silent
Night," and "Joy to the World." This is how most children
first learn of Jesus' birth. Music can build children's deepest
impressions and clearest visions of a spiritual Christmas if
we make sure they understand the lyrics. Music opens the
door to the heart. But to really have their full power, the
songs must be more than background music. Those songs
are heard more today than they ever have been, so put the
spotlight on them.

What's more, because carols and Christmas standards
are revived and embraced annually, they are literally time
machines. Our personal favorites take us back to a point
where we can revisit a special memory. When we hear just a
few familiar strains, suddenly we are back there, surrounded

by the warmth of that almost forgotten special moment. Music brings memory to the present.

The instant I hear "O Holy Night," I'm transported back to a small church in rural Illinois. It's Christmas Eve. I can see big, wet snowflakes and feel the chill in the air. I'm again a teenager listening to the incredible soprano voice of a young woman wrap her spirit around the words of this old French holiday standard. Thanks to this memory, even if it's eighty degrees outside, there's a sudden chill in the air and snow is falling. It's Christmas, and the spirit of the song is alive in my heart. Just as it did all those years ago, that song still elicits wonder and joy as it reminds me of the real meaning of this time of year and brings to mind the blessings found while sharing the holiday with friends and family. Surely each of us has a song that triggers a similar memory.

This magical musical element of Christmas is not new. It didn't begin with the invention of the iPod, the record player, or even the radio. Music has been a part of Christmas celebration from the very beginning. In Luke 2:13–14, the shepherds heard the very first holiday carol: "Suddenly a great company of the heavenly host appeared with the angel, praising God and saying, 'Glory to God in the highest heaven, and on earth peace to those on whom his favor rests.'"

Imagine how this choir of angels must have touched those humble men. The men were so moved, they left their jobs with great haste and rushed to a manger. And after seeing the babe, what did they do? They returned to their fields and sang of the wonders they had seen. I'm sure this event was a central focus for the rest of their lives. The tune and lyrics they heard that night were never forgotten. But that was just the beginning of the story of how music became an important part of the holiday.

Two hundred years before anyone officially recognized Christmas as a holy day, churches were singing of Jesus' birth. One song held such great power that the early church leader Telephorus issued an edict in AD 130. He ordered that after reading Scripture about Christ's birth, each congregation should sing the words "Gloria in excelsis Deo." Like the shepherds, these pioneering Christians were echoing the message of the angels.

Historical documents reveal that by the third century, this practice of singing Christmas songs was employed by all churches throughout Europe and the Middle East. It seems that even then, music was the key to making the Christmas season more spiritual. More than sermons could, early carols brought Jesus' birth to life, evoking the Christmas story in a way that touched not just the mind but also the heart.

By the Middle Ages, caroling was a part of many cultures. Ancient holiday songs were performed first by professional troubadours and later by bands of amateur singers. Through music, these people were spreading the good news and reaching more lost souls than the preachers of the era. These performers were vital tools in teaching the Christmas story and providing words and tunes that all could understand

and remember. And with the advent of organized cantatas and oratorios, the power of music grew even deeper in scope and message.

Perhaps no traditional song embraces the musical spirit of the season as does one written by Josiah Holland and Karl Harrington. One day, while reading one of the bestselling books of the 1800s, Harrington discovered a memorable piece of a poem, written by Holland, that was aflame with vigor and energy. As he read it, he was awed. He later wrote in one of his many diaries and journals, "This piece needs to be sung by Christian voices everywhere!"

Inspired, the songwriter picked up a pen and began to compose the music. When he finished his new tune, "There's a Song in the Air," he provided the world a glimpse of what the shepherds must have experienced as they listened to the angels.

There's a song in the air! There's a star in the sky!
There's a mother's deep prayer and a baby's low cry!
And the star rains its fire while the beautiful sing,
For the manger of Bethlehem cradles a King!

There's a tumult of joy o'er the wonderful birth,
For the virgin's sweet Boy is the Lord of the earth.
Ay! the star rains its fire while the beautiful sing,
For the manger of Bethlehem cradles a King!

In the light of that star lie the ages impearled;
And that song from afar has swept over the world.

Every hearth is aflame, and the beautiful sing
In the homes of the nations that Jesus is King!

We rejoice in the light, and we echo the song
That comes down through the night from the heavenly throng.
Ay! we shout to the lovely evangel they bring,
And we greet in His cradle our Savior and King!

"There's a Song in the Air" is more than music; its notes carry the spirit of Christmas. It is bright, uplifting, and hopeful. It provides us with the message that should ring in our hearts and spring from our lips. And it is just one of scores of songs that have the capacity to put your mind in a spirit of celebration.

As you consider all the carols you hear, which one is linked to your best memory of Christmas? What is the one musical moment in time when the spirit of the season first rang in your heart? Think about that magical moment. Embrace it. Then find a copy of that song and listen to it again. As that old memory comes back to life, join the chorus and sing. Pledge to start every day thinking of or listening to that song and remembering the special moment it preserved from your Christmas past. Do this one thing, and this Christmas will be as joyful as the one you experienced so long ago. The holiday season will also suddenly be warm, meaningful, and filled with a glow that most miss simply because they don't listen to the lyrics of the music all around them.

Music fuels the soul and calms the spirit. Music is

universal. Christmas music is timeless. By putting a song in your heart, you become more like the angels who brought the news of Christ's birth to earth, and like the shepherds who left their flocks to honor this new King. By having a song in your soul, you join with the earliest Christians in the melody of faith. By tying that song to a memory, you connect with your childhood and can see the real innocence and wonder of the season, usually lost on adults. Many things bring Christmas to life, but for most, music is the key to unlocking the passion of the season.

Don't think of Christmas carols as background noise. Listen to the words, embrace the message, and feel the wonder of the season. By putting a song in your heart at the beginning of the holiday season and making a conscious effort to keep it there, you allow yourself to be swept into the kind of excitement that filled those who heard the angels and witnessed the first Christmas. Isn't that the kind of joy you want to feel and share with others? You can have it. It's just a song away.

A Shortcut to the Spirit of the Season

Dig out your Christmas recordings, be they CDs or MP3s. Many cable and satellite systems also have special audio channels that play only Christmas songs; tune in to one. And listen to the music.

Day 5

Escaping the Inner Scrooge

Several years ago in eastern Tennessee, I was watching a Christmas-themed production. One of the songs written for the presentation was called "Bah, Humbug!" The humorous number was performed by a quartet of store clerks who hated the holidays because of all the extra work assigned to them during this special season. Written in a tongue-in-cheek style, the number captured the mood of so many I see at Christmastime. To this day I still laugh when I think about it. Yet if you go into almost any crowded store in the world, you'll find this "Bah, humbug!" attitude hanging over shoppers like a bad mood.

Far too often, a majority of people caught up in the hurried nature of the season, carrying long lists of things to do and places to be and items to buy, reflect the mood of Scrooge and the "Bah, Humbug!" clerks. They say, "Merry Christmas" as they gripe their way through the whole month of December. Rather than enjoy the holiday season, they can't wait for it to be over.

Our mood is deeply affected by our environment, and at times we don't have the power to control what's going on around us. But we do have control over how we respond to a situation. If we embrace the joy of the Christmas season, we defeat the Scrooge mood.

I'm often caught in traffic jams, bumper-to-bumper vehicles going nowhere. For years I spent the time looking at my watch and pleading with the cars in front of me to move. As seconds rolled into minutes, I grew angry. By the time I was on my way again, I was often so angry that for the rest of the day it affected the way I responded to others.

Then one day I discovered the blessings of being stuck in traffic. Not moving gave me a chance to look around and see sights I had driven by a hundred times before but never noticed. It gave me an opportunity to hear a few more Christmas carols on the radio and to think about a project I was working on. I discovered that being forced to slow down or even stop allowed me time to plan my week and rework ideas. Stuck in traffic, I had the chance to grab a few deep, relaxing breaths I would otherwise never get during my stressful day. In a real sense, traffic jams became an opportunity to take inventory and offer thanks for my many blessings. When I started looking at the slowdown of a traffic jam as a gift, I realized I was not only happier but also more productive.

Christmas is a month-long traffic jam. Everyone seems to be in a hurry. There are lines on the highway, in the stores, and on the sidewalks. Let's face it: we are all going to be stuck in a line sometime during this season. Rather than absorb the frustrations of others and develop their hostile attitudes, we should live the message found in that old song "Put on a Happy Face." The best way to start this process is by saying a short prayer. Thank the Good Lord for the chance to look around as you wait. It's amazing what you'll see that will make you smile, laugh, and even remember good times.

In Jesus' final days on earth, his life was filled with demands. His disciples peppered him with questions. Huge crowds lined his path. Many asked for healing or a favor. With so many pulling at him in so many different ways, and with so much of what he was saying misunderstood, Jesus would have been justified in having a "Bah, humbug!" attitude. If he had been like most of us, he would have kept his jaw clenched and his eyes focused on the road in front of him. Yet Jesus took in the wonder of the world. He stopped to visit, to heal, and to offer words of comfort. By doing this, Jesus spotted one of the Bible's most unforgettable characters.

When Jesus and his followers entered the city of Jericho, it must have looked like a parade. People were everywhere, shoulder to shoulder, all the way up and down the city's main street. The shortest man in town was a tax collector named Zacchaeus. A curious fellow, he wondered what all the commotion was about. Unable to see, he climbed into a tree. When Jesus saw him, he called out to him. "Zacchaeus, come down immediately. I must stay at your house today" (Luke 19:5).

The lesson for us in what Jesus did that day is especially important at Christmastime. We need to look around, see the wonders God has placed around us, reach out to others with the greetings of the season. When we do, we will not only bless but also be blessed.

In 1932, RCA recording artist and songwriter John Jacob Niles was the toast of Broadway. He could claim some of the bestselling records in the United States. Thanks to his fame, he had everything anyone could want. He was in every way a star. Yet in the midst of the excitement found only in the New York theater district—or the Great White Way, as it was then known—he missed the Appalachian Mountains and the slower pace of life he had enjoyed as a child. Just when it seemed everyone wanted to hear the great Niles, he walked away from the city's crowded streets and adoring crowds, in search of a place that would give him time to stop, to look, and to listen.

One cold winter's day in North Carolina, Niles was people-watching as folks in a poor community went about their daily life. As he took in the scene, one voice ever so faintly beckoned. Searching the street, his eyes honed in on a tiny girl, sitting by herself on a bench. Unaware that she had an audience, the child, dressed in hand-me-down clothes, was softly singing a song Niles had never heard.

Approaching the little girl, he inquired about the song's origin. She explained it was just something her mother had taught her. When Niles asked her to sing it again, the rosy-cheeked girl smiled and repeated the ballad's short, simple verses.

That song has since been heard around the world. Because Niles took a step back from his busy life to look and listen, he discovered "I Wonder As I Wander," a gift that not only blessed him but also has blessed millions of others:

I wonder as I wander out under the sky,
How Jesus the Savior did come for to die.

To fully appreciate all the wonders the season has to offer, we must face the holidays with the mindset of a child. Study preschoolers looking at a parade or viewing holiday lights. There is wonder in their expression and rapture in their eyes. And why not? They are seeing these sights for the first time. What a lesson for all of us.

As you venture out each day during the Christmas season, look at the world through childlike eyes. Traffic won't frustrate you; it will fascinate you. See the beauty in even the most simple decorations. And as you stand in line with other shoppers, experience the joy of realizing that for a change, millions are thinking of others more than they are thinking of themselves.

A change of attitude can do wonders. This isn't a time to rush; it's a time to savor. Enjoy the time you are forced to wait in line. Take a deep breath. Look around and study the faces of those around you. Focus on people who are relishing every moment of the season. Be like Christ. Reach out to those in need. Take time to offer a word of encouragement. And smile. Smile at those who seem to be at their wit's end.

This is the day to evict Scrooge from your Christmas celebration and erase the words "Bah, humbug!" from your vocabulary. Now is the time to view each mundane task as an opportunity to see something new or touch someone with holiday joy. Whenever it seems there is too much to do or too much being asked of you, stop, listen to the music in the air, and you will hear something uplifting that is a part of the season. Embrace that moment, and you will breathe new life and joy not just into your Christmas but also into the Christmas of everyone you touch.

~~~~~~~~

A Shortcut to the Spirit of the Season

One of the best ways to slow down is to take a walk. Walking gives you an opportunity to look around in a deliberate way and see things you miss speeding by in a car.

DAY 6

TRIMMING THE TREE

Nothing says Christmas like an evergreen tree. Of all the symbols of the holiday, it is the one we see most often. The story of the tree is one we should not just know but also share. Without this understanding, putting up the tree might just become another unwelcome chore rather than an exercise in love and faith. For your holidays to be full, rich, and rewarding, you need to shine a new light on your tree.

A few years ago I was answering questions about Christmas traditions on a radio program in Colorado Springs. One of the first queries came from an angry man. He vigorously explained his belief that the holidays had become so commercialized, no one thought of Christ's birth even on December 25. He then made an interesting observation: "Almost all of our Christmas traditions sprang from pagan traditions, and because of their roots, these symbols are flawed. Therefore the church should throw out any and every thing that did not have its roots in the Christian faith."

After momentarily considering his point of view, I posed a simple question: "Sir, have you always been a Christian?"

He quickly answered, "No. I wasn't saved until I was sixteen years old."

"How old are you now?" I asked.

"I'm in my thirties."

I then gently made an observation that put his view of Christmas into a uniquely Christian perspective. "Then for half your life you were not a Christian. If you follow your thinking on Christmas symbols like the tree, then we should toss you and me out of the church because we both have some pagan roots."

For a few seconds the phone line went silent as the caller considered my line of reasoning. Finally he said, "I hadn't thought of it that way."

The fact is, we all have lives that existed before we acknowledged God. No Christian was born a Christian. Accepting Christ changed our lives. At the moment we were saved, many of our past experiences took on new meaning. Many of our darkest sins even helped explain our journey into the light. God has the ability to use our past life experiences — even those rooted in what some would call pagan rituals — to enhance our own perspective and faith. And that brings us to the roots of the Christmas tree and why it's a holiday symbol that can reflect the depth of Christ's love for us.

Long ago evergreens were held in awe by Viking warriors. These powerful men knew winters that were long and harsh, in which many living things did not survive. During these bleak days, almost all plant life ceased to exist, and many animals starved to death. Stranded outdoors, a man could freeze to death. Yet in these horrid conditions, the evergreen not only survived; it thrived. Its vitality was so great, it seemed nothing could harm it. Because of that unique strength, the tree was seen as a source of mystery and power. Vikings prayed to their gods that they could be as strong and resilient as the fir tree.

When early Christian missionaries began explaining faith to these feared warriors, they used the evergreen as an example of God's undying love. They told the Vikings that even in their bleakest and darkest days, Christ would be with them. Their faith, like the evergreen, would survive every test. By putting this Christian lesson into a visible context, the missionaries helped thousands understand the love of God and the sacrifice of his Son. Yet the symbol of the evergreen and its tie to faith were not limited to Scandinavia.

In the seventh century Saint Boniface, an English missionary, came across a trio of men gathered around a huge oak tree in central Europe. One man was holding a small boy who had been chosen as a sacrifice to the god Thor.

Boniface raced up to the old tree and struck the trunk with his fist. The mighty oak shuddered and fell to the ground. As the dust settled, a tiny fir tree became visible just behind where the oak had stood. Boniface pointed to that little sprout and explained that the evergreen was the Tree of Life and stood for the eternal salvation offered by Christ. He also pointed to the triangular shape of the fir tree and explained that the three points represented the Father, Son, and Holy Ghost. Over the centuries, Boniface's "sermon" would be used thousands of times by missionaries all over the world. Long before the printing press was invented, the evergreen became the first Christian "tract" used in witnessing.

The evergreen would remain a symbolic teaching aid for missionaries and pastors for centuries, but it wasn't until the 1500s that people began to tie it to Christmas. Someone in Latvia brought a fir tree inside a home and hung it upside down from the ceiling. Perhaps this was done so the tree could be used as an illustration of faith, but soon everyone was doing it, though in time the tree was moved from the ceiling to the floor. The next important holiday transformation came when Martin Luther added candles to his tree to symbolize the light brought to the world by Christ's birth. That started another trend, and within a few years men and women were affixing homemade decorations to the branches. Finally, in the 1840s, when Queen Victoria put up a Christmas tree in Buckingham Palace, the entire world got caught up in evergreen fever.

With these historical events, the tree became an important facet of the holiday season. Yet with this transformation, much of the original symbolism of faith was lost. To make your Christmas more powerful, go back to the tree's Christian roots.

Knowing the way the evergreen was used to help lead the lost to faith can help keep your focus on the real reason why we celebrate Christmas. Every Christmas tree you see will be a reminder of the power of faith. That alone should make viewing Christmas trees a much more moving experience. Through sharing this story with your family and friends, you will spread the special, original meaning of the Christmas tree, which is the evergreen's connection to missionary work and reaching out to others. In fact, if your tree becomes a symbol of a love that will not die, it can be one of the greatest reminders of the gift God gave us in that humble manger. Furthermore, this understanding will create a door to sharing that good news with others.

Even if you don't feel like embracing the evergreen as the early Christians did, the Christmas tree is still much more than just a decoration. Think of it as a tie to the past. Each year, millions of us retrieve old decorations that have been carefully stored in boxes. Often, using these ornaments generates vivid memories of past Christmases. Thus, like few other things, the tree brings to life the love and wonder of former holiday seasons. Suddenly loved ones who have passed away are with you again. You feel their spirit and remember their warmth and love. In this way, the Christmas tree reunites us with our own family tree.

There is an element of strength that comes when you hang an ornament that once belonged to a grandparent. Just placing this trinket on a branch allows you to not just recall special memories of Christmases of old but to also introduce a new generation to someone they might never have met. By telling your children stories of family ornaments, you build a bridge to the past and preserve memories of those who came before. Yet the connection not only reaches backward; it goes forward as well.

Decorating a tree is a way to build a bridge to the future. New ornaments, chosen by children and grandchildren, allow those generations to display their interests in a unique way. A decade from now, these young people will see the decorations as a window back to their formative years, and you and past generations will be a part of the scene that's revealed. The tree's branches hold so much more than meaningless baubles. They hold symbols of love and signs of growth. A Christmas tree connects generations.

The tradition of the tree is strongest when shared. Decorating should not be a solo act. If that means you have to wait until loved ones can gather, be patient and wait. To make the most of the experience, include everyone, from the oldest to the youngest, and make the decorating fun. Too many see decorating the tree as a chore. Remind yourself that trimming the tree is a special time that unites a family in a meaningful way.

Day 6 ★ *Trimming the Tree*

In today's media-driven world, we all need to remember that decorating a tree is not a contest to see who can best match the styles in design magazines. Those "professional" trees might reflect today's fashion trends, but they don't have the warmth, wonder, and connectivity found on a "homemade" tree. Don't go for perfection; aim for unity and a reflection of family members' personalities. Encourage everyone to tell a story from Christmas past as they work together to create a tree that holds the decorations collected through the years. Don't rush the process. Let the decorating flow at its own pace. If it takes hours, treasure every minute.

In the early part of the twentieth century, presents were small enough to be tied on the Christmas tree. This tradition is worth reviving. Find little gifts for children and place them on the tree, the way your grandparents or great-grandparents would have done. As the kids look for their presents on Christmas morning, you can tell them stories about the history of different family ornaments.

The tree is the gathering place in your home, the first thing that catches the eye, so let it truly reflect your family and your faith. Make this facet of your Christmas as bright as the star atop the tree, and you will bask in the glow of a season filled with faith and love.

Finally, make the lighting of the tree an experience to remember. Make it a family tradition, gathering everyone together the first time the tree is lit. If you have to keep the lights unplugged for a few days as you wait for everyone to arrive, do so. The evergreen is a holiday symbol of homecoming and family; thus the anticipation of finally lighting the "love" lights is worth the wait.

To get the most out of your Christmas tree, don't look at it as a sideshow; see it as a treasure with special meaning for the season. Let the trimming of the tree open the vault to stories of past holidays. Create new memories that will live on for future generations. You might even sing a verse of the wonderful old carol about this great holiday tradition.

O Christmas tree, O Christmas tree,
Thy leaves are green forever.
O Christmas tree, O Christmas tree,
Thy beauty leaves thee never.
Thy leaves are green in summer's prime,
Thy leaves are green at Christmas time.
O Christmas tree, O Christmas tree,
Thy leaves are green forever.

A Shortcut to the Spirit of the Season

Boxes of animal crackers used to have a string handle, because the boxes were once used as decorations on Christmas trees. Animal crackers are cheap, everyone loves them, and hanging a few on your tree might bring a few smiles from kids of all ages.

DAY 7

EARNING YOUR WINGS

During the time between Thanksgiving and New Year's Day, angels seem to be everywhere. You can see them on rooftops, printed on Christmas cards, hung on trees, placed in elaborate yard decorations, and even used as symbols for charity fund drives.

Why are angels such an important part of Christmas? Probably because they are such an essential part of the Christmas story. After all, it was the angels who explained to Joseph, Mary, and the shepherds what was happening. How would these humble individuals have known what to do or where to go if these heavenly beings had not served as their guides? Angels are woven into the Christmas story, and Jesus' life story, in a way that is both spiritual and dynamic. Remember, it was an angel's voice that gave us this familiar greeting: "Do not be afraid. I bring you good news of great joy that will be for all the people. Today in the town of David a Savior has been born to you; he is the Messiah, the Lord" (Luke 2:10–11).

Many people grow up with the belief that angels are always watching out for us. I feel that this attitude is mainly due to the way angels were portrayed during that first Christmas. Who wouldn't want to be around a being with such grace, beauty, compassion, knowledge, and power? This is the type of person everyone would want on their team. Since that time two thousand years ago when shepherds were shocked to find angels in their midst, millions have longingly looked to the heavens during moments of crisis, hoping an angel would come to guide them.

Though we should look to angels every day of the year, it is especially during the holiday season when angels can be role models to us. If, over the next few days, we attempt to live our lives more as Christ did, we will automatically live out his commands to touch "the least of these." In that way, we will also be embracing the spirit of those who trumpeted his coming.

Perhaps one of the best modern and easy-to-understand examples of angelic behavior can be found in the Hollywood classic *It's a Wonderful Life*. Though not a financial success when originally released in 1947, over time this Jimmy Stewart film has become a most beloved treasure of the Christmas season. The world's adoration for this movie is in large part because of its theme that each of us has the power to change the world. The movie shows that by just being here and taking part in our day-to-day lives, we make the world a very different place than it would have been if we had never been born.

In *It's a Wonderful Life*, the angelic figure is somewhat of a misfit. On the surface he seems nothing like the graceful, wise, and beautiful creatures described in Scripture. Yet perhaps director Frank Capra portrayed Clarence this way to give us a clear look at the story's real angelic role model.

When a bumbling Clarence reviews George's life, showing him how different the world would have been without him, we discover that George is a man who reached out to help the least of those in his world. George's faith and sacrifices blessed others. Even though he didn't recognize it, that was why his life was so wonderful. In a real sense, George reflected the true meaning of Matthew 25:40: "Whatever you did for one of the least of these ... you did for me."

The story in *It's a Wonderful Life*, as well as the stories in scores of other holiday movies, TV shows, and bestselling books, proves that people want to believe in angels. They need the assurance that someone is looking out for them. They need to know that someone cares. They need to know that their lives have made a difference. In today's often cynical world, filled with so much greed and what seems to be little real caring, it is time to discover, as George Bailey did, that we can and do make a difference when we serve others in a special way.

Start the process by living the words of the angel found in Scripture: "I bring you good news of great joy" (Luke 2:10). Consider what these words mean to you and to the world. How different would this earth be had God not sent his Son? It is time to trumpet that good news.

Christmastime is the season when the world seems to lay aside misunderstanding and embrace a hope for peace. In the Franco-Prussian War, the Civil War, and even in World War II, enemies quit fighting to celebrate Christmas Day. This shows just how powerful the season is. And while you may not be a president, a king, or a general, God has placed in your hands the ability to make others feel that same power, grace, and peace today.

You can be the person who makes a joyful impact on this holiday season and on each day of the New Year. When you realize this, you will find so many ways to live out this new mission. Here are a few suggestions as to how you can earn your wings.

We all know someone who is alone, sick, or shut in. Pick up the phone and call them. Drop by for a visit. Deliver a meal. Find something they need and give it to them as a gift. If they don't have a tree, offer to decorate a small one for them. The best gift of all is to give them some of your time. Showing someone that you care lifts their spirit and makes their Christmas brighter. Just taking a few minutes to help a lonely person will greatly bless them, and it will bless you in ways you cannot imagine.

Discover the real joy in serving others. Volunteer with your family to spend a few hours at a soup kitchen or at a clothing or food drive. You are one phone call away from making this kind of action a reality. The hardest part is taking the first step and making that call. By helping to care for those who have very little, you are recognizing how much you have been blessed.

This is a busy time of year for almost everyone. Another way to reflect the spirit of Christ is to call your local school to ask if volunteers are needed to help with a holiday program or a classroom party. Schools, both private and public, look for those who can help. Your offer might open the door for you to become a friend or mentor to a child who needs some guidance and support.

Hospitals and children's homes always need extra help this time of year. A few hours of volunteer time can ease an employee's load and help give a sense of holiday peace and joy. Your caring presence can also spread the real joy of the holidays to those who are bedridden.

Show your appreciation to those who provide a service to you and others all year long. Everyone needs to feel appreciated. Take a snack to a group of workers. Many stores are so crowded during the holidays that employees barely have time for a break. Your thoughtfulness in providing a batch of holiday treats spreads the joy of the season. The impact is real. Your action lets others know you recognize their hard work. A card of thanks takes only a few minutes to write but means a great deal. Bring the true Christmas spirit to those who are overloaded by its demands.

One of the easiest things you can do is at your fingertips. Call one person who made a difference in your life. Tell the story of what happened, and let them know you think of them as someone God sent to touch you. Can you imagine what that would mean to this person? Knowing they changed your life is one of the greatest presents they could ever receive. It might be just what that person needs to again reach out to others.

Recognize others as they reflect this kind of spirit. Thank them for their loving, unselfish gifts. Make sure they know that they are appreciated, that their sacrifices are really impacting lives. This will encourage them to continue in their work.

To remind yourself to daily reflect the message and hope the angels brought to earth so long ago, focus on a specific Christmas carol that carries this theme. There are many, including "Angels from the Realms of Glory" and "Hark! The Herald Angels Sing." Perhaps the easiest to remember, as well as to sing, is one of the oldest: "Angels We Have Heard on High." Start each day with one of these songs on your lips, and you might discover that your soul is ready to fly.

Angels we have heard on high,
Sweetly singing o'er the plains,

And the mountains in reply,
Echoing their joyous strains.

Chorus: *Gloria in excelsis Deo,*
Gloria in excelsis Deo.

Shepherds, why this jubilee?
Why your joyous strains prolong?
What the gladsome tidings be,
Which inspire your heav'nly song?

Chorus

Come to Bethlehem and see
Him whose birth the angels sing;
Come, adore on bended knee
Christ the Lord, the newborn King.

Chorus

See within a manger laid:
Jesus, Lord of heav'n and earth!
Mary, Joseph, lend your aid,
With us sing our Savior's birth.

Chorus

When I sing this song, my soul is aflame. Though the words are simple, the message is strong. Think of the millions whose voices have embraced this carol. This is a song that resonates all over the globe. What it says to me and has said to others for centuries is that what happened so long ago is still happening now. Christ was born, but more important, he is alive.

As Christmas draws near, begin now to become the messenger who trumpets this season to everyone around you. You can be that special person who brings the spirit of the holidays to life. You can live out Matthew 25:40. Not only will your holidays become brighter, but you may decide to continue this positive attitude in the New Year. Those who know the true joy of giving find that they too have been blessed with a wonderful life. And isn't that really what we all want for this Christmas and beyond?

Webster's Third International Dictionary defines an angel as "a divine winged messenger." While accurate, this definition fails to describe the warmth experienced by those who have been touched by an angel. As you live out a real spirit of giving, with warmth and kindness, someone might point to you this Christmas and say, "That's the one God sent to touch my life."

~~~~~~~~

A Shortcut to the Spirit of the Season

Take the time to focus on one section of Scripture during this busy season. I suggest you make it Matthew 25:34–40. Leave your Bible open to these verses, and you will be reminded daily of the most important mission you can have, during the holiday season and throughout the entire year.

Day 8

Having an Impact on Others

About ten years ago I went to my mailbox on a warm day in June and discovered that one of our close friends from Colorado had sent us a Christmas card. I was so taken aback by the timing of the delivery, I immediately checked the postmark. I figured this holiday greeting had been lost in the mail, and someone at a post office had just discovered it. But no, it had been mailed just three days earlier. Thus, the card that arrived at the beginning of a long, hot summer was somewhat of a mystery. It included holiday greetings and a handwritten update for the year—last year.

Several weeks later I happened to touch base with Shelly,

the sender, and the subject of the summer Christmas greeting came up. Shelly explained that she had written and addressed her cards in early December. She placed them in the car to take them to the post office. While she was running errands, the cards slipped under the seat. Later, when she didn't see them, she assumed one of her kids had dropped them in a mailbox. Six months afterward, while cleaning out her car, she discovered the forgotten holiday greetings. Rather than worry about the timing, she simply mailed them.

Shelly's cards made quite an impression. She received calls from scores of friends. Everyone told her how much they enjoyed her belated holiday greetings. Thanks to the response generated by that late mailing, a new tradition was started. Now, a decade later, Shelly still waits until summer to send out her Christmas cards. Quite by accident, she discovered what we all need to know—Christmas cards can have a great impact.

When I was a kid, we received stacks of Christmas cards each year. These simple cards were a sincere connection from one family to another. They meant a great deal to us. After reading the cards, we would set them out in places where visitors could easily pick them up, enjoy the varied designs, and read the special notes inside.

What I learned as a child, and what I still cherish today, is that Christmas cards are fun to get. Each has the power to touch us in a special way. Just receiving a card is an uplifting experience. Each card you find in the mailbox means that someone cared enough to take the time to remember you.

Yet in spite of the good they can do, Christmas cards in our modern age are no longer on the "must-do" list. Many people today do not mail Christmas cards. The main reason: it takes too much time.

The irony is that Christmas cards were created by a man who saw their potential as a time saver. Sir Henry Cole, an English knight of the realm, sent the first Christmas card in 1843. Besides his job as an assistant at the public records office, Cole was a well-known author and a publisher and editor of children's books. He was director of the London Museum and the founder of the *Journal of Design*. He was a close friend of Queen Victoria and Prince Albert. The prince was so impressed with Cole's energy and accomplishments, he often said, "When you want steam, you must get Cole!" Sir Henry Cole had both money and power.

With the demands of his varied jobs and his busy social calendar, Cole keenly felt the pressures of time. His mailbox was overflowing with correspondence from both friends and business associates. The stack grew higher and higher, and he grew further and further behind in his replies. One day Cole picked up a rigid piece of paper. Studying it, he bent it in half, folding it so that it resembled a small book. Fascinated with the possibilities, he opened the paper. As he looked at the blank pages, he recalled how in his younger days he had once been asked to draw a holiday scene as a gift for his parents. In a burst of inspiration, Cole realized that by combining that long-ago school assignment with a message on this thick, folded piece of paper, he had a solution to his annual December problem—answering letters. Thus the Christmas card was born.

Cole had a friend paint a picture of a holiday scene to print on one side of the paper and added "A Merry Christmas and a Happy New Year to You" on the inside. He then had a thousand cards printed, which he personally signed and mailed.

This simple card started a fad. An industry was born. Within two years, sending Christmas cards became the way thousands of English families shared holiday greetings. In fact, with the cards and the national mail service so affordable, the British postal department found itself hard-pressed to keep up with the volume of mail created by the new custom. They had to hire extra workers. Hence another Christmas tradition was born.

Cole's reason for sending out cards in 1843 still holds true today. A Christmas card is a fast and easy way to communicate greetings to someone dear to you. It takes far less time to write an address on an envelope and put on a stamp than it does to make even a short phone call. Cards are relatively low-cost and easy to find. Even at today's rate, mail delivery is still reasonable.

When I was young, I loved going to my grandparents' home during the holidays. I used to look over all the cards they received and read the messages penned to Grandpa and Grandma Shell. Through these notes, I came to understand how many people my grandparents had touched with their acts of kindness and friendship. I also developed a keen curiosity about the places all over the world from which these cards had been mailed.

Christmas cards can be beautiful, funny, sentimental, or spiritual, so take a few extra moments to match your cards with those on your list. This personal element means the most. Select cards that not only reflect your personality but will have special meaning to your recipients. Include a brief note that explains your feelings for the person to whom you are sending the card. Maybe you can thank them for something they did for you. Or write about a blessing from your own life. Thanking people for their kindness and sharing good news was how Paul began his correspondence to the early churches. The apostle's letters give us a framework for showing our appreciation.

If you don't feel you have time to send the old-fashioned type of holiday greetings, then email or even text a holiday message. By remembering others this way, you are letting them know that the spirit of love—so often lost during the year—is still part of their world. By sending a message of love in your Christmas cards, you are reflecting Christ on his birthday.

Sir Henry Cole, who was deeply concerned about the plight of London's poor, would no doubt be overjoyed to know that not only has his invention brought happiness to millions, but it has also been used to raise funds for everything from cancer treatments for children, to feeding the starving in Third World nations, to funding research to end diseases.

Thus, another way to reflect the spirit of Christ during this season is to purchase cards that raise money for a charitable cause. That way, your Christmas greetings not only lift the spirits of ones dear to you but also help needy people you will never meet. The card you send that highlights a special cause might pave the way for others to support that cause by making them aware of the need.

One of my wife's favorite modern Christmas songs is the Carpenters' "Merry Christmas, Darling." This beloved standard begins with the line "Greeting cards have all been sent." Through this line, Frank Pooler and Richard Carpenter emphasized this meaningful tradition of Christmas.

A Christmas card touches others on a personal level. Easy to find, a card is one of the least expensive presents you can give during the holidays. Add a personal message and you help make this holiday season much brighter for others. No matter when it arrives, in early December or even in the middle of summer, a Christmas card warms the heart in a special way. So dust off an old tradition and make it a vital part of your holiday season.

~~~~~~~~~~~~~~~

A Shortcut to the Spirit of the Season

Want your cards to stand out? Send cards that are antiques. Many antique malls have boxes of Christmas cards that are more than fifty years old. These are very different from cards used today. Or make your own cards. It's easy to find a book with plenty of ideas and the instructions for you to make cards, with or without a computer.

DAY 9

TURNING A
BLUE CHRISTMAS WHITE

Holidays can be the loneliest time of the year. While some people are gathering with friends and family to unwrap presents and make cherished memories, millions are locked inside their homes with no one to share in the joys of the season. Suicide is the solution for some on what is supposed to be the most joyous day of the year. In December the truth of the old song lyric "One is the loneliest number" is especially true.

During the height of the rock-and-roll era, Elvis Presley had a huge hit that addressed the sadness of being alone at Christmas. You might smile each time you hear Gene Autry sing of the red-nosed reindeer, but whenever you hear the loneliness in the lyrics of "Blue Christmas," it almost breaks your heart:

> *Decorations of red on a green Christmas tree,*
> *Won't be the same dear, if you're not here with me.*

For those who are always surrounded by family on Christmas Day, the message in that mournful Christmas classic is a completely foreign thought. Yet for the millions whose holidays are solitary events, Christmas really is colored only in blue. Just remember, you have it in your power to make this season a great deal warmer, brighter, and more meaningful for yourself and others.

When I was a child, we always had a huge family gathering, encompassing three to four generations, at my grandparents' home in Salem, Arkansas. Often the family meal would include a person I didn't know from the community. You see, Grandma Shell always saw to it that none of her neighbors were alone at Christmas. If one of us brought an unannounced guest to the party, Grandma would say, "Always got room for one more." And she did too. She prepared extra just in case someone dropped in. The more people we had around the table at Christmas, the better the day became.

Look around and identify those who are going to be alone on December 25. In truth, they aren't hard to find. There are many people whose family cannot get home for the holidays.

These folks might live on your block or go to your church or work with you. Some of your friends are probably in this group. Colleges have students from foreign countries. Many children of American missionaries serving overseas have no place to go during the holidays. Consider setting an extra place at your table this year. Invite someone who otherwise would be alone to join you for your Christmas celebration. Add a present or two to the bounty already under your tree. When you have Christ in your heart, there is always room for one more. Sharing the joy of the season always magnifies its impact and creates memories that live on through the years.

What if you are going to be alone for Christmas this year? What if you know that while everyone else is gathering in family groups, you'll have to wish yourself a merry Christmas? Don't settle for a solitary holiday. Take charge and change that bleak prospect.

Start with the basics. Christmas is a holiday based in faith. Most churches have either Christmas Eve or Christmas Day programs. Some have both. Find out where these churches are and the times for worship. Ask what type of service each conducts. A few even offer Christmas dinner for those who otherwise would be alone. Pick one or two that fit your special interests or needs. Don't limit your choice to simply the church you know (although by attending your church, you connect with close friends and experience the warmth created by your church family). By visiting a new congregation or denomination, you'll experience new traditions that will give you a fresh perspective on the way others worship. No matter where you go, you will discover that worshiping with others, praying with them, and singing carols with them lifts your spirits. You are reminded that with the Lord in your life, you are never alone.

Consider making Santa your role model. If you wonder why you should follow in the footsteps of a red-suited elf, consider this: except for a few reindeer, the jolly old fat man is alone every Christmas. Not even Mrs. Claus is with him as he goes on his rounds. But he doesn't allow that to keep him from spreading great cheer. With that in mind, look for places where you can deliver gifts of joy this year.

Think of the people who have to work on December 24 and 25 because the service they provide must continue every day of the year. They include firefighters, police officers, hospital staff members, members of the media. Spend a part of Christmas Eve or Christmas morning making holiday treats for those who have given up their holiday to serve others. Deliver your gifts in person. Enjoy seeing the response as you become a reminder of the true spirit of this special season.

Another way to make a difference at Christmas is by visiting a nursing home or a hospital. Seek out those no one visits. For many years my kids and I used to take our collie to a nursing home at Christmas. Our visit brought more smiles than you can imagine. Call to get a list of special gifts you can take with you. Watching someone open your gift can become a memory that will last a lifetime. The hours you spend reaching out to the sick or elderly not only brightens their day but also enriches your life.

Find an organization in your area that has a special program for the needy on Christmas Day. Volunteers are needed to help feed the homeless, the abused, the shut-in. Through this kind of ministry you are no longer alone. As you work with others to prepare food or serve meals, you are reaching out to "the least of these" and fulfilling the true meaning of having a merry Christmas.

Talk to folks at work or at church or at your civic club who are going to spend Christmas alone. If they are interested, organize your own party. You can make it a simple potluck meal or an elaborate feast with turkey and dressing and even gifts. But what's most important is that a group of lonely souls are coming together for a celebration. By creating this unique "family," you push the blue out of the holiday season and bring light to others' Christmas as well as to your own.

If none of the options listed in this chapter will work for you, and you know you are going to be alone this Christmas, don't give up. Count your blessings. Know that those blessings often came to you through people. Make a new kind of Christmas list, writing down the names of those who have touched you in a special way. List their telephone numbers, and try to find a way to contact the ones who are going to be away from home during the holidays. On Christmas Day call each person on your list. Thank them for what they did. Your thank-you will not only surprise them but also likely touch them deeply. You will have provided an unexpected and mighty present while filling your own world with the joy of giving. And at the end of the day, as you reflect on these brief conversations, you will realize that you are never really alone.

A blue Christmas can be turned into a day of wonder if you vow not to feel sorry for yourself and if you pledge to create a Christmas Day that will bless others. Make your plans early, and you will have a holiday to look forward to, one that will create special memories for you and for others.

~~~~~~~~~~~~~

A Shortcut to the Spirit of the Season

Most of us take for granted being able to call a loved one. But some people can't afford the expense of a long-distance phone call, especially if the ones they love live overseas. Calling cards with prepaid minutes are available in many stores. Give one as a gift to someone who otherwise would not be able to talk to a friend or family member on Christmas.

TAKING A NEW LOOK
AT MISTLETOE

In our modern world, mistletoe is looked upon as the "kissing plant." It is seen as a way to steal a smooch from someone. While the plant does bring a bit of humor and romance to Christmas, that is pretty much where its effect on the holiday begins and ends. No one takes mistletoe seriously.

The history of mistletoe, and the story of how it became a part of the holiday season, puts a new spin on this old Christmas tradition. In 1 Corinthians 13 the apostle Paul gave us one of the most beloved pieces of writing that can be found in either the New or Old Testaments. Though these words were not composed as a link to the Christmas story, perhaps no Scripture ever written better reveals why God sent his Son to earth. When Paul examines the noise and confusion created by the world and compares it with the peace and wisdom found in faith, a great truth is revealed: all of what Christ sought to teach us is based on love.

If I speak in human or angelic tongues, but do not have love, I am only a resounding gong or a clanging cymbal. If I have the gift of prophecy and can fathom all mysteries and all knowledge, and if I have a faith that can move mountains, but do not have love, I am nothing. If I give all I possess to the poor and give over my body to hardship that I may boast, but do not have love, I gain nothing.

Love is patient, love is kind. It does not envy, it does not boast, it is not proud. It does not dishonor others, it is not self-seeking, it is not easily angered, it keeps no record of wrongs. Love does not delight in evil but rejoices with the truth. It always protects, always trusts, always hopes, always perseveres.

Love never fails. But where there are prophecies, they will cease; where there are tongues, they will be stilled; where there is knowledge, it will pass away. For we know in part and we prophesy in part, but when completeness comes, what is in part disappears. When I was a child, I talked like a child, I thought like a child, I reasoned like a child. When I became a man, I put the

ways of childhood behind me. For now we see only a
reflection as in a mirror; then we shall see face to face.
Now I know in part; then I shall know fully, even as I
am fully known.

And now these three remain: faith, hope and love.
But the greatest of these is love.

1 Corinthians 13

So what does this have to do with mistletoe? In ancient
times mistletoe was viewed with great awe. It was considered one of the world's most mysterious living things. In
the midst of winter, during the harshest storms and freez-
ing temperatures, during days when it seemed that nothing
lived, this small flowering plant thrived. No one could understand how that was possible. It was seen as a miracle, and
stories were told concerning the origins of this evergreen
plant.

Today it seems strange that a botanical leech, a plant that
sucks its life out of another living organism, could inspire
such awe. Before the advent of science, people believed that
trees died in the winter. They didn't see them as going into
a dormant state; they saw them as being dead. Thus, a new
green plant springing forth out of winter's dead wood was
a miracle. Mistletoe was once considered a sacred and noble
gift that represented life, hope, and security.

The plant was held in such awe that Vikings would stop
a war if they found themselves fighting under trees where

mistletoe grew. A host of other societies soon adopted this rule as well. Mistletoe became not just a symbol of peace but also a marker placed by God which demanded that nations find a way to create real peace.

As the legend of mistletoe grew, it soon took on another role—that of protector. If the plant could stop hate and end senseless killing, some felt, then it might also help fend off disease. Mistletoe was cut from trees and nailed or tied over the doors of homes and barns. It was even placed over babies' cribs. Some used it during funeral services, as a sign that death might have killed the body (the tree), but it hadn't killed the soul (the mistletoe plant).

In England, mistletoe was used in evangelism. Pastors and priests led people to Christ by framing the Savior's life in a context the English peasant could understand. Missionaries painted the world before Christ as a barren and hopeless place filled with war and pain. It was Christ who brought light and hope. When the world did not accept him and he was crucified, the light and hope seemed lost. According to legend, mistletoe grew from the cross, representing Christ's triumph over the grave. To Christians, the plant became a symbol of life after death and of faith so strong that it could sustain and grow even in the midst of darkness.

Christians across Europe seized this new view of mistletoe and posted the plant over their doors to show the world they believed in the love God had sent through his Son. Thanks to this expanded view, many came to see the green plant as a symbol of unity and love. When a courting couple passed under the plant, they had to stop and kiss. The belief was that if they did, God would bless their love. Soon the "kissing plant" was even held over a bride and groom during the wedding.

Several hundred years ago mistletoe was adopted as a part of the Christmas season, representing four special elements of Christianity: love (God sent his Son because of his love for us), hope (Jesus brought hope to the world), peace (knowing Christ brought peace to the heart), and faith (the combination of these three created faith).

Adding mistletoe to our decorations celebrates its Christian roots. With mistletoe hanging over the door or in our home, we have a symbol that can remind us of the great love God has for us. It also reminds us to put that love into action in our thoughts, our words, and our deeds.

Embrace mistletoe in two special ways. First, remember the history of the plant and why it came to be a part of our holiday tradition. This will remind you that faith is alive in even the darkest days of the year and that love is at the heart of Christmas. Second, tell others how the plant is a representation of God's love for us and a symbol of eternal life and the resurrection. In this way, mistletoe becomes a vehicle for witness.

Love is alive at Christmastime. After all, Christmas is a love story. Become a beacon of light in a world of darkness.

Let your Christlikeness show through your eyes, your expression, and your touch.

As it says in John 3:16, "God so loved the world that he gave his one and only Son, that whoever believes in him shall not perish but have eternal life." Rather than seeing mistletoe as just a symbol of romance, this year view mistletoe as a reminder to celebrate God's love by letting that love shine through you. You will make your Christmas brighter and bring joy to everyone you meet.

~~~~~~~

A Shortcut to the Spirit of the Season

Reclaim the tradition of mistletoe in your home. The plant can be found in trees all over the world. There's probably some not far from your home. Mistletoe is also readily available at stores during the holidays.

DAY 11

SHOPPING LIKE A WISE MAN

As we celebrate the birth of Jesus, we recognize that this is an exciting time filled with joy and wonder. Smiles and laughter surround us. Children are especially filled with a great sense of wonder during this season. If we take on the attitude of a child, we will find Christmas to be a wonderful gift just waiting to be unwrapped.

Scientific studies have proven that people who are in high spirits and smile a great deal not only live longer but also have a much higher survival rate when battling severe illness. Those who manage stress rather than having stress manage them are happier and more relaxed and take far less prescription medicine. Many of those who choose happiness over worry seem to embrace the words of Christ as he told his disciples not to worry about earthly things. Those who don't fret the small stuff, like traffic jams or checkout lines, seem to get a whole lot more done than those who are constantly looking for shortcuts.

At no time is this relaxed attitude more important than during the Christmas season. One thought to keep in mind during the holidays is, "Don't worry, be happy." If you are running so fast that you're having problems catching your breath, sit down, take a deep breath, and look around. This simple act is usually the first step in realizing that you are in a winter wonderland filled with happiness and hope. It won't make your list any shorter, but keeping your perspective will help you get the most out of this season.

During the holidays, shopping usually gives people the greatest stress. For most, the biggest problem is how to find a present that will really be appreciated. Before you fret over your list, consider the pressure the wise men must have felt when they looked for a present for the Son of God. What these visitors from the East went through might help you put your Christmas shopping and travel into perspective.

> After Jesus was born in Bethlehem in Judea, during the time of King Herod, Magi from the east came to Jerusalem and asked, "Where is the one who has been born king of the Jews? We saw his star when it rose and have come to worship him."
>
> When King Herod heard this he was disturbed, and

all Jerusalem with him. When he had called together all the people's chief priests and teachers of the law, he asked them where the Messiah was to be born. "In Bethlehem in Judea," they replied, "for this is what the prophet has written:

"'But you, Bethlehem, in the land of Judah,
     are by no means least among the rulers of Judah;
for out of you will come a ruler
     who will shepherd my people Israel.'"

Then Herod called the Magi secretly and found out from them the exact time the star had appeared. He sent them to Bethlehem and said, "Go and make a careful search for the child. As soon as you find him, report to me, so that I too may go and worship him."

After they had heard the king, they went on their way, and the star they had seen when it rose went ahead of them until it stopped over the place where the child was. When they saw the star, they were overjoyed. On coming to the house, they saw the child with his mother Mary, and they bowed down and worshiped him. Then they opened their treasures and presented him with gifts of gold, frankincense and myrrh.

Matthew 2:1–11

As we examine the stresses of the first Christmas shopping excursion, let's consider the fashion in which these men chose their gifts. They didn't just go out and grab the first thing they saw at the local market. If we examine these first three holiday presents, we discover there was a purpose in each selection.

At the time of Christ's birth, gold was even more highly prized than it is today. For a man to give a gift of gold meant that the receiver had to be a loved one or someone of high standing. No one would have given gold to a child unless that child was from a royal family. The wise men knew that Jesus was royalty—the king of the Jews. In addition, they may have been given insight into his future work. Perhaps they somehow knew that this gold would be used to support the most important work the world had ever known. Thus the gift may have been meant not only to honor a king but also to help provide for his future.

When they picked out the frankincense, they were planning ahead as well, it seems. This was a gift given to only a special person. The tree this spice comes from was considered so scarce that only those pure of heart and mind were allowed to come near it. The sap was used as an ingredient in anointing oil. Frankincense was also burned during special offerings. The wise men may have sensed that frankincense would be needed during this child's mission on earth. Once again, it appears, their gift centered on both the present and the future.

Myrrh was a rare and costly resin used in burial ceremonies. In a sense, it was a strange gift for a child. This would be like bringing a coffin as a present to a baby shower.

Possibly, this spice was chosen because these men understood that Christ was here not just to live for them but to die for them as well.

The important thing to realize about the wise men's gifts is that each was carefully chosen with great purpose in mind. While few of us will be giving gold, frankincense, or myrrh this Christmas, we need to put the same kind of careful thought into every gift we buy. If a person is worthy of making your shopping list, don't just buy something on the spur of the moment. Consider the person and what they really could use. Put yourself in their shoes. What will be their reaction when they open your gift? If you consider this, you'll be much more likely to pick out a gift they will treasure for a lifetime. And that is much easier to do if you're in a good mood.

To go shopping, you usually have to make a trip. Many hate getting out into the real world and making the trek to the stores before Christmas. Once again, think back to the wise men. They made a long journey. It took them weeks or even months. They no doubt fought the elements, had to deal with the danger of bandits, and spent hours riding under a hot sun and suffering through cold nights. Their trip was not easy. Still, I believe these men must have enjoyed the experience and taken time to look around and see the sights and make memories that they talked about the rest of their days. You can do that as well. Rather than keeping your eyes straight ahead, note the decorations, the excitement, and the beauty of the Christmas season. As you shop, take time to look up, to look around. With all that is new each Christmas, you will likely see something you'll remember for many years to come.

During the Christmas season, all of us have a lot of things on our plate and a lot of places to be. So the question becomes, are the holidays going to manage your attitude or are you going to use a good attitude to help you manage the holidays? The latter will ultimately serve you better.

How do you begin this attitude readjustment? How can a modern person develop the attitude of an ancient wise man from the East? Start by doing something as simple as singing a song.

I recently read a medical report on CNN noting that people who listen to music at least once a day are happier than those who don't. Music must really make folks happy during the holidays, considering how much of it is in the air! I have long felt there is nothing better than Christmas music, and I have to believe everyone knows at least one Christmas song. As you look at your long "to do" list, perhaps you should be humming your favorite carol. This could be kind of a holiday version of whistling while you work. When you start to feel stress, remember that song you love and hum it silently, in your head. Within the first few notes of the tune, more than likely, the joy of the season and the calmness in your soul will return.

Step two in the process of becoming as joyful as the

season is simply turning your frown upside down. If you're smiling as you go through your errands, things that get in your way or slow you down won't bother you as much. View each step of Christmas as a grand adventure in which you can let others see the spirit of the season in your face and in your actions. Sit down, observe the decorations and the beauty, watch the shoppers, help others who seem to be lost. Remember, by simply being kind, you can be an encouraging example and a positive influence. Your good mood will work like a ripple on a pond, and your smile will be passed on through those you touch.

Consider the song "It's Beginning to Look a Lot Like Christmas." In those lyrics there is a joy found in shopping, because you are buying something others want. Though the message is dated ("A pair of half-a-long boots and a pistol that shoots is the wish of Barney and Ben, / Dolls that will talk and will go for a walk is the hope of Janice and Jen"), the joy of finding just the right gift still rings true.

Finally, keep in mind what the wise men knew: a gift honors another person. A gift is a symbol of love and respect. Your attitude when you choose a gift will be reflected when the gift is opened. If you buy something thinking, "That will do," your present will reveal your lack of effort and concern. When you take time to consider the person and match your gift to them, your thoughtfulness will shine like a lighted Christmas tree on a dark street.

Make Christmas shopping fun this year by keeping a

song in your heart. Use the first gift givers as your role models. Your shopping will be less stressful, and you'll have a much more enjoyable holiday season.

~~~~~~~~~

A Shortcut to the Spirit of the Season

A book that will add something special to your holidays this year is *The Story of the Other Wise Man* by Henry Van Dyke, originally published in 1895. It's easy to find. In fact, you can read it online or download it from Project Gutenberg at www.gutenberg .org/etext/19608. It's a short book, about seventy pages. But the message is powerful and will no doubt put the season into sharp focus for you.

DAY 12

COUNTING THE TWELVE DAYS

Surprise! You only have a dozen days until Christmas Eve.

If you are like most people, you probably have a million things to accomplish in that brief time. So how can you keep a focus that allows you to really enjoy each moment of those days while tackling all your chores? With all the things on your "to do" list, coupled with the unexpected interruptions that will come into your life, how can you keep the reason for the season front and center over the next twelve days? It seems like such a challenge, but it only takes a few seconds and a single thought each day to change your whole perspective. These daily sticky note reminders just might be the key to having your most joyful Christmas in years.

Most people believe that the twelve days of Christmas

start either today or tomorrow and run through Christmas Eve or Christmas Day. Historically, the first day of Christmas is December 25 and the final day comes in the New Year, on January 6. If you consider this, then many old movies that have delightful Christmas scenes as an important part of their plot will make much more sense. In classic films such as *Christmas in Connecticut*, the tree isn't decorated until Christmas Eve. This is no mistake by the scriptwriters or director. For centuries the Christmas holidays didn't begin until the Christmas Eve service and did not end until the day of Epiphany, January 6, when gifts were opened.

I am not suggesting you buck the modern trend and hold off your tree decorating until Christmas Eve and your present unwrapping until January 6. We can't turn back the clock. But starting today, we can celebrate in a special way the twelve days of Christmas.

In the Dark Ages, churches in eastern Europe began to hold twelve days of worship services in which Christians were encouraged to focus on rededication and renewal. Each day's service focused on a different facet of worship. Much more than at any other time of the year, children were an important part of the presentations. For hundreds of years, the twelve days of Christmas were embraced in a worshipful and meaningful fashion.

Few today would commit to spending a dozen nights in a row in church just before Christmas. Yet there is a way to reflect on the blessings of the season and refocus on our faith that doesn't require us to leave home. And an old song can help us create the mood to do just that. When "The Twelve Days of Christmas" was written, the song was not viewed as the nonsensical ditty we hear today. The lyrics had a special meaning for those who sang it. By taking the original meaning of those verses and concentrating on one verse a day, we can re-create the kind of sharply honed Christmas focus that church members had centuries ago.

We all know how the carol begins: "On the first day of Christmas, my true love gave to me a partridge in a pear tree." That partridge is Jesus, the Son of God, whose birthday we celebrate on the first day of Christmas (remember that when the song was written, December 25 was the start of the season). Christ is symbolically presented as a mother partridge because that was the only English bird that would die to protect its young.

You can continue your countdown of the dozen days of the season by considering not just the birth of Jesus but his entire life. When you think of the ramifications of his life, you should be able to see the holidays with a much more spiritual view. Not only was he the Son of God, but he was also a man whose thoughts, lessons, and life still play an essential part in the world today.

On the second day, remember the two turtledoves highlighted in the next verse of the old carol. These twin birds represent the Old and New Testaments, the road map God has given us for each facet of our lives. No matter what our problems, we can find answers in the Bible. God's guidance is always at our fingertips.

On the third day, consider another kind of bird. The three French hens represent the three gifts God gives us on a daily basis: faith, hope, and love. Consider the message written by Paul in 1 Corinthians 13 on these three elements of our Christian walk.

On the fourth day, we focus on yet another set of winged creatures, the calling birds. These refer to the four Gospels—Matthew, Mark, Luke, and John—and the story of Christ's entire life. Read again the message found in these books. It tells us why Jesus came, what he taught us, and why he died. Take a moment to reflect on how much we owe to those who saved this story for us by way of the written word. These were men of great courage and wisdom. Just as they were used by God, you can be used by God.

On the fifth day of Christmas, we are given a precious metal in five gold rings. Gold was a valuable commodity in ancient times. The first five books of the Old Testament also were considered valuable. The stories in them are well known and give us a tie to people in many different parts of the globe. Our roots can help us come together with almost anyone, anywhere, at any time.

When you get to six geese a-laying, you will be halfway to your destination on your musical advent journey of faith. The meaning of the number six and why it is linked to eggs is simple. Each egg represents a day in creation, a time when the world was "hatched," or made by God. The creating process never ends. It repeats itself in each new generation. Give thanks for the generation we sprang from, and for our own generation, and for the next generation as well. Dedicate yourself to a week of living for the Lord.

On the seventh day of Christmas, the spotlight is thrown on swimming swans. These graceful, beautiful birds represent the seven gifts of the Spirit—prophecy, ministry, teaching, exhortation, giving, leading, and compassion. As you begin the second half of your countdown to Christmas, consider which of these seven gifts God has given to you. Then consider how you can use these gifts to further the goal of peace on earth.

In some ways, the eighth day of Christmas might well be the one that means the most to us. At the time this song was written, a woman who milked cows had the lowest and worst job in England. Yet Christ came for even the milkmaids. The eight maids a-milking represent those who, according to Jesus, are blessed: the poor in spirit, those who mourn, the meek, those who hunger and thirst for righteousness, the merciful, the pure in heart, the peacemakers, and those who are persecuted for the sake of righteousness.

With four days to go, picture nine ladies dancing. These are the gifts known as the fruit of the Holy Spirit, and they include love, joy, peace, patience, kindness, goodness, faithfulness, gentleness, and self-control. These are gifts offered to you. Vow to accept and use these gifts, and you will find that each day of this season and of the New Year will be more meaningful. God lives in you, and through your touch others can find this fruit.

On the tenth day of Christmas, focus on the ten leaping lords. This is the easiest gift to understand. The lords were judges. The focus is on the Ten Commandants, the Mosaic law that puts some order in life. By embracing these laws, you live your life as a positive witness.

Two days before your Christmas celebration, remember the eleven pipers piping. These represent the eleven faithful apostles who lived out the gospel message and fearlessly shared it with the world. Most gave their lives for their faith. Your world is much different because of these men. Your goal should be to live for the Lord as they did. Sharing the Word is much easier today. You can do it by speaking to others and by living out God's message in your actions.

On the twelfth and final day, the gift is twelve drummers beating drums. Your faith puts you in this band. Those who believe that the one who came at Christmas is God's Son can sing a song of salvation to the world. And that is really why we celebrate Christmas — to share the good news with others. It is time to remind others that Jesus is the reason for the season.

As you get ready to embrace the next twelve days the way Christians did so many years ago, consider one more element of the old familiar carol. Each verse contains the phrase "my true love gave to me." Who is this true love? It's

God. He is the one who gives us these twelve gifts of the season.

Remember that all the gifts found in this carol are available to those who accept Christ as the Son of God and as their personal Lord and Savior. Embrace that one element of this ancient song, and you are guaranteed a much more meaningful Christmas this year.

~~~~~~~~~~~~~

A Shortcut to the Spirit of the Season

Do you like to solve puzzles? Want to challenge your kids or grandkids this year? Have each one guess how much it would cost today to buy these special gifts. Google each item given in the twelve days of Christmas to find the cost. Several internet sites list prices for the current year. This exercise involves research, addition, and multiplication. Did anyone come close to the total cost of these gifts?

DAY 13

THANKING GOD
FOR THE MEMORIES

Other than Santa Claus, probably no one has traveled more at Christmas than the late Hollywood legend Bob Hope. For decades this incredible entertainer packed his bags and hit the road to personally deliver holiday greetings and cheer to American military personnel serving all over the globe. During World War II and throughout several other armed conflicts, those in uniform could be sure that if it was Christmas, they would likely get a visit from Bob Hope. He journeyed to every continent and stopped in places that literally were not on a map. He gave performances for crowds of thousands as well as for audiences whose members could be counted on two hands. He visited the battlefronts and the hospitals. And he rarely traveled alone.

Hope convinced scores of other top entertainers to give up time with their families to bring the Christmas spirit to men and women in the army, the navy, the air force, and the marines who were not going to get home for Christmas. The sacrifice he asked from these show business icons often included flying into areas where the entertainment troupe might well be in harm's way. Yet they went anyway; nothing seemed to stop them. In the face of bad weather and enemy fire, Hope and his company somehow made their appointed rounds and delivered special gifts that resonated long after they had left. By just being Bob and caring deeply about those who were serving their nation, he gave millions special memories they would never forget.

Hope's signature song was "Thanks for the Memories." Though it came to be associated with the holidays through his USO tours, it was never intended to be a Christmas song. In fact, it was not really meant to be a hit. "Thanks for the Memories" was just a throwaway number in the 1938 film *The Big Broadcast of 1938*. Hope, who had made only one other film appearance, was an afterthought as well, listed sixth in the credits. It was W. C. Fields who got top billing.

Though entertaining, the movie was a nothing and probably would have been quickly forgotten if not for the duet by Hope and Shirley Ross. When "Thanks for the Memories" won the 1939 Academy Award for best song, Hope's destiny seemed set. Within four years he was the biggest star on radio, was a top draw at the box office, and, through his USO tours, was giving millions memories to cling to during the toughest holidays of their lives.

Over the years, Hope received thousands of cards and letters from those who had been in the traveling road show's audiences, thanking him for giving them the best present they had ever received. These thank-you notes were from men and women fighting in theaters of battle around the globe.

What Hope and his troupe did was remind servicemen and servicewomen that they were loved, missed, and appreciated. As the performers worked their way through songs and dance numbers and jokes, Bob Hope and the others made it feel like Christmas, even when the stage was in the middle of a steamy jungle. Hope's tours brought a brief illusion of peace on earth and goodwill toward humanity to those whose whole focus was on fighting a war. He understood the caring we all need to express during the Christmas season.

Hope's gifts of time and talent touched hearts in a profound way. What he did on a large scale, we can do on a much smaller one. All it takes is a bit of time and effort. We can become more like Hope, just as others have been like him in our own lives.

We all have a talent. If you can sing or play an instrument, dust off those skills, make some calls, find a few others to join your troupe. Work out a few numbers and make an appointment to perform at a nursing home or veterans hospital to bring joy to those who can't get out during this holiday season. Consider how much these elderly members of our society, these silent and forgotten heroes, have contributed to our world. Some may have been in the audience when Hope made his tours. Your performance is sure to be rewarded with smiles as you play familiar and favorite tunes, bringing back memories of past Christmases. In that way, as you take the time to be with folks who might otherwise have been alone and forgotten, you will be like Bob Hope.

If you don't feel comfortable entertaining others, go to a nursing home or veterans hospital to spend some time with people who have no visitors. Take along a box of Christmas cards and some stamps and ask those you meet if they would like you to help them send holiday greetings to their loved ones. Or take the time to read something to a resident whose vision has faded. Select a book with interesting short stories. Ask those you visit about their favorite memories from past Christmases.

Your cell phone, especially if you have a program with no additional charge for long-distance minutes, is the perfect way to help someone reconnect with a long-lost friend or relative. After the call ends, stick around to hear stories about the person who was called, about the memories shared on this special holiday visit. Folks love to reminisce, even with a stranger.

Local newspapers and churches usually have a list of men and women who are serving in the military or as missionaries and won't be home this Christmas. Send a card with a word of thanks and a special holiday greeting to those who will be far away. If there is a story in the local newspaper that captures the holiday spirit, include it with your card. Take a few photos of the town's decorations and send them along. Like Hope on his visits, you are adding a touch of home to a faraway place. You are letting someone know that you care and that you appreciate their sacrifice.

Think too about others who in the past cared about you and made a difference in your life. It may be a friend, a relative, a boss, a coworker. Pen a few thank-you notes. The best way to remember who has deeply impacted your life is to take a few moments for reflection. What incident stands out in your memory?

A present, carefully chosen and given with love, can also form a strong memory. What were the best Christmas presents you ever received? I still recall in vivid detail getting an electric train and transistor radio as a child. On my desk I have a paperweight given to me by a special friend. There are probably a half dozen things you have received at Christmas that meant a great deal to you. These gifts were all chosen with care and given with love. Consider writing a thank-you note. Write what is on your heart and describe your memory of the present. Explain why that particular gift has been so important to you. A few years ago I wrote such a note to my grandfather. It so touched him, he kept it. The note was read at his funeral.

The impact of getting a thank-you note for a gift years

later is great. The giver probably will recall not only the present but also why you were the recipient and what it took to find the gift. The expression on your face when you opened it also may be a cherished memory. Wrap yourself in the warmth of feelings that once made your holiday special. Put pen to paper and send a thank-you for that treasured gift from the past. Your words of thanks will become an unforgettable present for someone who cared for you long ago.

As we immerse ourselves in the holiday season and recall days of old, we say, "Thanks for the memories" in both our words and our actions. You don't have to travel far to bring hope to others, to make a difference. You just have to make an effort. Like Bob Hope, you bring the joy of the season when you reach out to others and let them know they are appreciated and loved.

A Shortcut to the Spirit of the Season

Put a focus on service to others for this holiday season. Rent a DVD that shows highlights from Bob Hope's Christmas trips to entertain the military. Many of the entertainer's best moments from his trips can also be found on YouTube. Dig out old home movies or videos to bring back the magic of past holidays. Be ready to video highlights of this year's celebration to grow your bank of memories.

DAY 14

LETTING THE
HOLIDAYS SHINE

Vast numbers of special lighting displays are put up between Thanksgiving and December 25, thanks to a tradition that gives all of us a public way to share the story behind Christmas. These light displays are a brilliant and creative reminder of the reason for the holiday. They give us an opportunity to share the good news, to put what we believe on display. And this is a chance you don't want to miss.

You are the light of the world. A city on a hill cannot be hidden. Neither do people light a lamp and put it under a bowl. Instead they put it on its stand, and it gives light to everyone in the house. In the same way, let your light shine before others, that they may see your good deeds and glorify your Father in heaven.

Matthew 5:14–16

The light transforms us. Staying in the light keeps us focused on what we need to do during our time on earth. In fact, it is the light that sets Christians apart from others. We are told in the Bible that we are the light. And we are given the charge to take that light to the world.

The child born in a manger was the brightest light ever brought to a dark world. He remains that to this day. Therefore it should hardly be surprising that the dark nights of deep winter are brightly lit in the days leading up to the one when we celebrate Jesus' birthday. After all, since Christ is the light of the world, Christmas must be the brightest time of the year.

The first Christmas light was a star placed in the sky for the wise men to follow. It lit up the first Christmas in a grand way, announcing that God had come to earth. Can you imagine what that beacon must have looked like? It must have been something very special to prod men to leave their secure world and make a dangerous journey into a foreign land. That first Christmas light must have been dynamic and awe-inspiring.

For the next fifteen hundred years, the light brought to the world at Christmas was usually represented by candles burning at a church altar, in a home's window, or on a family's table. The leaders of the church as well as the most modest of parishioners shared in this holiday tradition. These displays were simple but meaningful symbols of faith. Today candles are still used to signify a wonderful spiritual aspect of the holiday season.

The great Protestant reformer Martin Luther generated the spark that would really light up the season. On a cold, clear December night five centuries ago Luther was walking home through a stand of fir trees. Starlight was filtering through the evergreen branches. He would later tell his family that the silence of the woods, combined with the beauty of the light reflecting off the snow-covered branches, brought him a great sense of peace. That experience inspired him to add something new to his family's traditional Christmas display.

Hurrying home, Luther tied several candleholders to branches of a fir tree that he and his children had already decorated with fruit and nuts. He then placed a small white candle in each holder, took a burning twig from the fireplace, and transformed the look of the Christmas tree forever.

Within a generation, placing candles on Christmas trees was an accepted and treasured custom throughout Eastern Europe. With the arrival of this holiday tradition, a new business sprang up as artists, working in both wood and metal, designed candleholders especially for use on a tree. By the middle of the 1800s, millions of homes all around the globe had candles on their Christmas trees, and thanks to this tradition, the holidays were literally glowing.

In 1879 Thomas Edison and his lightbulb changed the way America illuminated homes. Three years later one of his employees, Edward Johnson, decided to apply the concept to Christmas and created the first string of Christmas lights. Replacing candles with electric lights was such a revolutionary move, newspapers from across the country dispatched reporters to view the first tree decorated with colored lights. A story in the *Detroit Post and Tribune* reported that breathtaking display in great detail: "I need not tell you that the scintillating evergreen was a pretty sight—one can hardly imagine anything prettier. The ceiling was crossed obliquely with two wires on which hung 28 more of the tiny lights; and all the lights and the fantastic tree itself with its starry fruit were kept going by the slight electric current brought from the main office on a filmy wire. The tree was kept revolving by a little hidden crank below the floor which was turned by electricity. It was a superb exhibition."

Technology opened the door for the world to begin fully displaying what Christmas has always been about—light. An invention that changed the world also emphasized what the wise men knew: Christmas is light. What was true two thousand years ago is still true today: nothing reflects the glow of faith like the lights of Christmas. Nowadays Christmas lights seem to be on every street, beckoning from windows, rooflines, and lampposts. They come in different sizes and colors. They blink, twinkle, icicle, and cascade across our landscape. They are in stores, on homes, covering trees, and even outlining yards. Become more like Martin Luther. Take a deep breath, pause, and enjoy the lights. Don't rush by them. Savor the experience. Have a childlike attitude while looking at each display. Imagine you are seeing everything for the first time.

Don't just hold the light inside your heart and mind. If a display moves you, leave a thank-you note for those whose hard work helped remind you of the wonder of the season. Better yet, seek them out and tell them in person how their efforts have touched your heart. After all, sharing light with others is an unselfish act that brings joy. Remind the ones who have given you this gift that they are appreciated. But don't stop there.

My mother's mother always put only blue lights on her tree. Each time I see a blue light, I see my grandmother and think of her love for us grandkids. My father's mother had a large angel chime display. Whenever the candles were lit, the angels moved and rang the bells. Both of these women made light special for those who entered their world. You can too.

Find a way to shine a light in your world. Lights can be purchased inexpensively. Buy a few strands and make your home a beacon that will make people stop and look. Create a display that reflects your view of Christmas. You will have no idea how many you touch with your gift of light, but be assured that your selfless effort will have an impact. Your work might well be what puts someone's focus back on the real joy of the holiday. It might lead a person to Christ in the same way the star led the wise men to Jesus so long ago. Your display might be the road map someone needs to find the true meaning of the season.

This year, take another long-forgotten tradition to heart. For centuries children were taught that a candle on a tree represented a prayer that needed to be answered. When you see lights on a tree, pray for someone who has a need. Remember those who are suffering. Think of people who have no joy this season, who are facing a difficult issue. Let the lights prompt you to recall the problems of others and, when possible, help them carry their heavy loads.

In a very real sense, the glow of billions of Christmas lights reminds us just how much the babe in the manger has changed the world and is still changing the world. This holiday season, revel in the light.

~~~~~~~~~

A Shortcut to the Spirit of the Season

I received a flashlight when I was a child. My father liked to give them to small children. Not only can they light up a dark room, but they also can entertain a child's imagination in a magical exploration of the dark. As an adult, I see a flashlight as an opportunity to share the story of the light that came into the world on the first Christmas.

DAY 15

MAKING THE PICTURE PERFECT

This Christmas is not just about the now; it's also a bridge between past holidays and those of the future. One special and easy way to celebrate the past, present, and future is through photography.

It has long been said that a picture is worth a thousand words. When it comes to capturing special memories, this is true. A photograph has the power to take us back to another place and time. It refreshes the mind, toys with emotions, and makes the past reappear.

Like nothing else in the family scrapbook, a photograph is a magical connection to the past. When people look at pictures, they often pose questions. Those inquiries lead to stories that lead to more questions. Soon the past has been brought to life, and days of old are with you again. That is the dramatic and unusual power of photography.

For a while, video cameras took the place of still cameras at family gatherings. It is wonderful to see life presented by those moving images. But although video almost captures it all, it does not have the power to connect the way a still photograph does. When you freeze a moment, there is an intimacy that just doesn't exist in moving images. That's probably why you are now seeing fewer video cameras pop up at Christmas and a lot more still imaging taking place. A photo holds and even expands a moment. You can pick it up, study it for as long as you like, and see details you had not noticed before. A photograph is as user friendly as anything you will find at Christmas. It requires no technical skills or programming abilities to view it. Family pictures will make this holiday one you will never forget.

At the first Christmas, a couple traveled a long distance to return to the town of their family, and when they arrived at their destination, a new family member was welcomed into the world. Ever since then, the holidays have been a time when families gather, events happen, and special memories are made. In the old days, when all cameras used film, photo labs reported that there were more pictures taken at Christmastime than at any other time of the year. This is still true today—more photographs are taken—but as technology has shifted from film to digital memory, fewer photos are being printed. Many are just filed away on computer hard drives and forgotten. To make this Christmas memorable, record the moments with your camera and print the pictures.

Sharing your best photos is easier and more affordable than ever before. Several services on the internet allow you to design a photo book on your computer and order bound copies of your project in full color, delivered about a week later. Using page templates, you design the book, insert your photos, include written descriptions of what was going on in the various shots, list the names of those photographed, and add the dates the pictures were taken. Sharing your digital images by making a book will provide enjoyment for many years to come.

You need a plan to make the most of your photo opportunities. Begin by writing down the various events and gatherings you will be attending or hosting. Note those who will be at these events and make sure you get photographs of each person. Remember, people—not scenic sites or floral displays—make the most memorable photos, so take good close-ups of your loved ones.

Think like an old-time Hollywood photographer. These masters of film took scores of candid shots during the production of movies. They caught their subjects in action, relaxing between takes, and even playing games during breaks. Do the same. Take shots of people talking, laughing, unwrapping packages, arriving, leaving, playing games, playing in the yard. These images freeze action and capture memories. And remember the golden rule of photography: you can never take too many pictures.

For my family, Christmas wasn't Christmas unless we gathered on Shell's Hill in Salem, Arkansas. I have lots of pictures of the house and lots of group family shots, but I don't have a single image of my grandmother cooking our big meal. I also don't have any shots of the table filled with all the goodies she prepared or of our family sitting down to enjoy the feast.

When I look through the photographs of my own family holidays, it's as though I was never there. Don't make that mistake. The photographer needs to be in the shot, not just taking it. Give the camera to someone else from time to time. Get in the picture. Become a part of the action.

After you make plans for this Christmas, which includes buying extra batteries and making sure your camera goes with you at all times, think about past Christmas celebrations. In a scrapbook, picture album, or desk drawer, you probably have holiday photos that go back for many years. Look through them. Make them a part of this year's celebration. Identify the photographs you want to share with others. If your family will treasure a large group of the pictures you have collected from the past, take advantage of modern technology and create a book with those images.

When you're working solely with old snapshots, you'll have to convert them to digital images to use on a computer. If you have a scanner, you already know what to do. Otherwise, have the photos scanned into digital images. Maybe a friend or a relative has a high-quality scanner. Discount stores and office supply stores and photography stores offer this service. Once the images are scanned, you can create your book. As you put it together, include text that gives the who, what, when, and where details of the various photos. Add family stories.

Too often, old family photos become meaningless because no one remembers who is in the picture, where it was taken, or when. Antique stores often sell old family pictures that have been discarded because no one bothered labeling them. As you go through your pictures, turn them over and write carefully, in pencil, detailed information on the back. Be sure you don't press so hard that the writing leaves an impression on the front of the photo. Also, ink can bleed through the photo paper and ruin a picture. Future generations will thank you for this simple act, and odds are that your family pictures won't end up being tossed in the trash or sold.

Frame some special images and use them as a part of your holiday decorations. You will find that putting your pictures out for others to see will prompt stories of prior Christmases and give you a fresh look at past holidays. These images also connect one generation to another by keeping family traditions and history alive through the stories behind the pictures.

Elvis Presley had a big holiday hit single with a song called "If Every Day Was Like Christmas." A successful

Broadway show had a popular number entitled "We Need a Little Christmas." Both of these classic songs have lyrics longing for a holiday season that continues throughout the year. Find the best Christmas photos you have, frame them, and keep them up all year long. They will remind you of the joys of past holidays and bring others the Christmas spirit every time they see those photos.

Finally, look at the images of past holidays, and if you see one that might make a friend or family member smile, share it. It's easy to send photos via email. In these hurried and crazy days as we count down toward Christmas, an old memory preserved in a photograph can be a welcome surprise. If you have several photographic treasures, send one a day as a reminder that the real joy of the season is found in simple things like family, friends, and shared love. Your daily email will become a photographic advent calendar.

A photograph is a time machine that erases the years and makes old emotions seem fresh and alive. Don't miss the chance to record the events of this holiday season and, in the process, freeze time for future generations. By starting now, you can give yourself and your loved ones a clear record of why Christmas is such an important time for your family. Remember, a photograph, by prompting stories, ties together Christmas past, present, and future.

~~~~~~~~

A Shortcut to the Spirit of the Season

Turn a camera over to a few children to take photos showing what they really love about Christmas. These pictures, taken with the fresh eyes of youth, often provide new insights into the ways of children and what they view as special.

Day 16

Discovering the
True Spirit of Santa

How can you become a Santa to someone who is drowning in sorrow, hopelessness, and woe? First, realize who and what the red-suited man represents. To put this into sharp focus, take a trip back to another age by reading the story behind what well may be the most famous newspaper editorial of all time.

Every day, millions of letters are sent to newspapers around the country. Over the years, these "letters to the editor" have helped advance women's suffrage, civil rights, school reform, and a host of other dynamic movements. Carefully chosen words in letters have changed the course of history. But no letter ever penned to a newspaper's office has been read as many times or remembered as long as the one written by a young girl named Virginia more than a century ago. It was printed on September 21, 1897.

Dear Editor,

I am 8 years old. Some of my little friends say there is no Santa Claus. Papa says, "If you see it in *The Sun*, it's so." Please tell me the truth; is there a Santa Claus?

Virginia O'Hanlon

The letter could have been disregarded. It could have been dismissed as unimportant and tossed in the trash, but it was not. Those at the *New York Sun* found themselves troubled by what they read in the little girl's letter. None of them wanted to break Virginia's heart; all of them wanted to raise her spirits. Yet when asked to respond, the paper's top scribes shook their heads and begged off penning a reply.

Finally, Virginia's letter fell onto the desk of veteran reporter Francis P. Church. He too was taken aback. This son of a Baptist minister was dedicated to telling the truth and nothing but the truth, in its raw, unvarnished form. Would he be moved by the words of a child about a whimsical fable?

Church was a tough, seasoned man who had covered the Civil War for the *New York Times*. He had seen death by the tens of thousands and experienced anguish and hardship like few men ever had. His life had been filled with grit and loss, and this clearly showed in his writing. He pulled no punches as he wrote graphic stories exposing the price of murder, the cost of lies, and the ramifications of corruption.

So how was a man who dealt with those great issues going to deal with a child's simple question? How could he delicately explain that Santa was not real? How could Church write the truth and not break the girl's heart? The gap between truth and compassion seemed too wide to bridge. He put off answering Virginia's letter and prayed for the wisdom of Solomon.

Church spent some time walking the streets of New York to observe the city's Christmas decorations and soak in the cheery mood of those anticipating the holidays. From the financial district to the sidewalks of Broadway, from the Bronx to Harlem, from Central Park to Battery Park, he could see Christmas everywhere, and all that he saw was wonderful. In a city where it was often dog eat dog, people were looking out for each other. Men were reaching out and giving others a helping hand. What Church witnessed on the streets during those cold winter walks didn't just lift his spirits; it proved to him that there was something special afoot during the holidays, something that didn't exist at any other time of year. Suddenly he had the answer to Virginia's question and to his own prayers.

What Church wrote still resonates today. Just reading his words might give you a new view of the special role Santa Claus plays at Christmas. You probably will also see the potential you have to change the course of this holiday season in the modern world. Church wrote,

> Virginia, your little friends are wrong. They have been affected by the skepticism of a skeptical age. They do not believe except they see. They think that nothing can be which is not comprehensible by their little minds. All minds, Virginia, whether they be men's or children's, are little. In this great universe of ours man is a mere insect, an ant, in his intellect, as compared with the boundless world about him, as measured by the intelligence capable of grasping the whole of truth and knowledge.
>
> Yes, Virginia, there is a Santa Claus. He exists as certainly as love and generosity and devotion exist, and you know that they abound and give to your life its highest beauty and joy. Alas! how dreary would be the world if there were no Santa Claus. It would be as dreary as if there were no Virginias. There would be no childlike faith then, no poetry, no romance to make tolerable this existence. We should have no enjoyment, except in sense and sight. The external light with which childhood fills the world would be extinguished.
>
> Not believe in Santa Claus! You might as well not believe in fairies! You might get your papa to hire men to watch in all the chimneys on Christmas Eve to catch Santa Claus, but even if you did not see Santa Claus

coming down, what would that prove? Nobody sees Santa Claus, but that is no sign that there is no Santa Claus. The most real things in the world are those that neither children nor men can see. Did you ever see fairies dancing on the lawn? Of course not, but that's no proof that they are not there. Nobody can conceive or imagine all the wonders there are unseen and unseeable in the world.

You may tear apart the baby's rattle and see what makes the noise inside, but there is a veil covering the unseen world which not the strongest man, nor even the united strength of all the strongest men that ever lived, could tear apart. Only faith, fancy, poetry, love, romance, can push aside that curtain and view and picture the supernal beauty and glory beyond. Is it all real? Ah, Virginia, in all this world there is nothing else real and abiding.

No Santa Claus! Thank God! he lives, and he lives forever. A thousand years from now, Virginia, nay, ten times ten thousand years from now, he will continue to make glad the heart of childhood.

Just reading this letter, whether for the first time or the hundredth, should prove to you the need to keep the spirit of Santa alive. In so many ways, embracing the spirit of St. Nick reflects some of the lessons taught by Christ during his walk on earth. Consider this: Santa forgets no one, he reaches out to all, he is unselfish, he is cheerful, and he is always dependable. When no one else cares, he does. The qualities Church wrote about are what we need to reveal whenever we touch the lives of others in the twenty-first century.

What is the best way to carry on the spirit of the jolly old elf? First, get involved in the season. Don't hide from it. Don't push it aside. Note what Church did. See the way people are reaching out to help others during this time of the year. Magnify your blessings by sharing them. If you have a neighbor who is having a tough time, find a way to help. Maybe you can secretly pay a utility bill or provide groceries.

Do you know a family who cannot afford to purchase Christmas presents for their children? Discreetly discover what the children want. Become Santa. Buy those presents and find a way to secretly get those gifts to the family. If you never let them know who filled their wish list, the children and the parents will feel wrapped in the holiday spirit and its magic.

In many cities, Christmas drives to meet the needs of poor families have embraced a song made famous by the country group the Oak Ridge Boys. This rather recent addition to holiday music was not intended to become a Christmas classic, but with its message of the precious gifts we find in each new generation, "Thank God for Kids" resonates during the holidays like few other songs. Many, after listening to the words of the song, have been moved to action with the giving spirit. So listen to "Thank God for Kids" again and vow to make sure forgotten kids know that someone cares.

The great missionary doctor Albert Schweitzer once told a group of college students, "I don't know what your destiny will be, but I do know that the only ones among you who will truly be happy are those who have sought and found how to serve."

Through serving others in great need, we become more like God. Start this practice now as you prepare for the holidays.

Santa's DNA can be traced back seventeen hundred years to a man named Nicholas. The giving spirit of that early church leader was so strong that it continues touching children all over the world. In German Santa's name might be Weinachtsmann (Christmas man); in France, Père Noël; in Russia, Father Frost; and in England, Father Christmas. But no matter where he is or by what name he is known, all of us should emulate his mission.

You still have time to prove to others that there is a Santa Claus. Become someone's secret Santa. No matter where you live, you can be this year's answer to Virginia O'Hanlon's question. You can prove that Santa is a vital part of the giving spirit of Christmas. It all begins with a loving touch.

~~~~~~~~~

A Shortcut to the Spirit of the Season

A wonderful song by the country music group the Statler Brothers, called "I Believe in Santa's Cause," sets the tone for the hundreds of thousands of men and women who spend time ringing bells for charitable purposes. Volunteer for even an hour. And thank those dressed in a Santa hat for their effort in support of Santa's cause.

DAY 17

PUTTING AWAY YOUR ANGER

Anger is one of the most common emotions that reveal themselves during the holiday season. In the madcap countdown to Christmas Day, it doesn't take long to find something to be mad about. What is amazing is how trivial most of these things can be.

I have seen folks go into a rage when stores use the term "Xmas" or "Holiday Tree." Other seasonal triggers that cause anger include long lines at cash registers, traffic jams, crying children, empty shelves in stores, and Christmas lights that won't work. Combine a few of these and many lose control. Anger erupts again a few weeks after the holidays when the credit card bills arrive.

Much that is good at Christmas is missed due to anger.

My grandmother used to say, "If you can't do anything about it, then it's not worth worrying about." While I kept hearing that saying in the Ozarks, it is almost biblical in its wisdom and value.

Consider what Proverbs 15:1 says: "A gentle answer turns away wrath, but a harsh word stirs up anger." Most of us shout when we are angry. We take out our rage on those around us. We look for ways to justify our anger. When we're in an express checkout lane, we count the number of items in the cart of the person in front of us. We want him or her to be one over the limit, so we can point out how rude that is. When a checkout clerk has to call for a price check, the delay raises the frustration level for everyone. We look for someone to blame. The same is true after a traffic accident. Someone yells, "Why weren't you watching what you were doing?" or even "You're an idiot!" Even though such anger does not reflect a Christian spirit or a true holiday attitude, people find ways to rationalize it.

There is another way. Take a deep breath. Quit looking at the clock. Look for something that lifts your spirits and calms your nerves. It takes little effort. Look for a child who is excited at seeing decorations for the first time. Look for something that reminds you of a special memory from a past Christmas. Listen and you might hear a song that helps you return to the joy of the season.

Proverbs 21:14 says, "A gift given in secret soothes anger." There are many gifts you can give. Saying something nice to the one who seems to be causing your rage can do a great deal to diminish your anger. Find a way to talk to the person who has a few too many items in the express lane and say something positive about one of the items. As you wait together, ask about holiday plans. Thank a clerk for helping you complete your shopping. Give a verbal bouquet to those you meet. Results will be twofold: your rage won't have a chance to develop, and you will spread cheer by being a positive witness.

Patience is an important gift we can give ourselves. When you're always in a hurry, mistakes happen. Anger builds. You miss seeing wonderful things. But you can change that. As you begin your day, ask yourself, "Why am I in such a hurry?"

Four days a week I ride my bike to the post office. I thought about doing this for years, but I didn't because I felt that taking the bike would cost me too much time. Finally, when the price of gas went over three dollars a gallon, I aired up my tires and jumped on my bicycle. Several things happened when I made this move.

When I was driving my car, I found myself getting impatient with lights as well as with road crews and delivery crews. I would feel my blood pressure rise when I couldn't find a parking place. The lines at the post office and bank bothered me too. As a driver, I constantly checked my watch and rushed from place to place. Worst of all, I noticed nothing and rarely spoke with anyone.

When I hopped on my bike, my mind slowed down. During the five-mile round trip, I smelled flowers, fresh air, and special scents that came and went with each new season. I greeted folks working in their yards and even stopped and talked with the road crews. I noted the beauty of gardens, of houses that had been repainted, and of the window displays in shops. And I never had a problem finding a parking space. When I arrived at the post office, I no longer minded the lines and even enjoyed striking up conversations as I waited.

A couple weeks ago I observed a man frantically driving his truck around the block as he looked for an empty parking spot. I was sorting my mail when he rushed into the post office, opened his box, and raced back to his truck. Five minutes later I arrived at the bank just as he hurried in to get in line. He and I finished up about the same time. I was a mile from my home office when I pulled up to a stoplight just as the man in the pickup truck did. He anxiously drummed his hands on the wheel while I talked to a man working in his garden. The man in the truck and I had both arrived at the same place at the same time while accomplishing the same things, but a slowed-down attitude gave me a much different view of the world.

What I have learned from my bike rides is that I enjoy the trip a lot more and arrive back at my office relaxed and in the right frame of mind for work. The trip takes just a couple minutes more than driving. In other words, just slowing down and having some patience has brought an improved attitude to my life. At Christmas, slowing down brings even more incredible things into your world.

Christmas is a time of wonder and joy. Even with a lot to do, we need to slow down and enjoy the splendor of the holiday. That simple change of attitude—taking a step back and not being concerned about things you can't control—allows you to enjoy things you would have otherwise missed.

The choice is yours. What will you dwell on in the days leading up to Christmas? What emotion will reveal your faith and your witness? Keep in mind that Christmas is about love, compassion, and peace on earth, and there will be no place for your anger to take root.

A familiar Christmas song written more than a century and a half ago can help you keep your emotions in check and your focus on the real meaning of the holiday. This is a song we sing each year, but knowing more about it puts life into a special perspective.

Henry Wadsworth Longfellow is one of America's greatest poets. He was already an internationally acclaimed poet and the proud father of five when he wrote such classic poems as *Evangeline*, *The Song of Hiawatha*, and *The Courtship of Miles Standish*. He was famous all over the globe, the toast of Harvard. Then, in one instant, tragedy hit.

Longfellow's wife was lighting a match, and her clothes caught fire. She burned to death. Before he could regain his stride from that loss, his nineteen-year-old son was wounded in the Civil War. On Christmas Day 1863, Longfellow was

angry. He saw nothing in the holidays worth celebrating.
His writing reflected this emotion:

> *I heard the bells on Christmas day*
> *Their old familiar carols play,*
> *And wild and sweet the words repeat*
> *Of peace on earth, good will to men.*

> *And thought how, as the day had come,*
> *The belfries of all Christendom*
> *Had rolled along the unbroken song*
> *Of peace on earth, good will to men.*

> ...

> *And in despair I bowed my head*
> *"There is no peace on earth," I said,*
> *"For hate is strong and mocks the song*
> *Of peace on earth, good will to men."*

> *Then from each black, accursed mouth*
> *The cannon thundered in the South,*
> *And with the sound the carols drowned*
> *Of peace on earth, good will to men.*

> *It was as if an earthquake rent*
> *The hearth-stones of a continent,*
> *And made forlorn, the households born*
> *Of peace on earth, good will to men.*

If Longfellow had allowed his anger to completely shut

himself off from the season, he would have likely never again found the joy of the holidays. Christmas would have remained a day he dreaded. In the midst of his writing, he got up from his desk and walked to a window, where he saw happy, hopeful faces in the street. He heard men, women, and children yelling out "Merry Christmas!" In the distance he heard carols being sung. Suddenly the bells that caused him such great anger sounded different. Returning to his desk, he picked up his pen and wrote two more verses.

> *Then pealed the bells more loud and deep:*
> *"God is not dead, nor doth He sleep;*
> *The wrong shall fail, the right prevail*
> *With peace on earth, good will to men."*
>
> *Till ringing, singing on its way*
> *The world revolved from night to day,*
> *A voice, a chime, a chant sublime*
> *Of peace on earth, good will to men.*

The last stanza is the one we need to keep in our hearts as we go through our list of holiday chores. We need to remember that if Christ were forced to wait in line, he would not get angry. In fact, he would probably offer words of encouragement to all around him. He would see the wait as an opportunity to share good news.

Adopt this concept this year by always saying, "God bless you" and "Merry Christmas," not as an afterthought but as if you really mean it. It will lift you and scores of others as well. Treat even the moments when you are forced to wait as a gift that allows you to look around and note the wonder of the holiday and to speak words of encouragement and cheer to others. Take a deep breath; look at all the sights around you. You will experience more joy from this blessed season and become an instrument of "peace on earth, good will to men."

～～～～～～～～～～

A Shortcut to the Spirit of the Season

Give yourself a symbolic gift that removes the anger you feel during the Christmas season. Write down all the things that upset you about the holiday. Place the list in a box, wrap it like a present, and place it under the Christmas tree. Vow to keep those holiday anger issues out of your life. Open this present to yourself in January, after all the things that usually upset you are over.

DAY 18

EMBRACING THE GIFT OF COMMERCIALIZATION

One of the most beloved secular holiday songs was introduced to the world more than five decades ago by a former barber. When Perry Como first sang "It's Beginning to Look a Lot Like Christmas," the song's lyrics focused on the signs of the season found only in December. But now the holiday rush seems to get started earlier and earlier each year. In the last two generations, Christmas has evolved from a sprint to a marathon. With a week more of holiday activities left on your calendar, you may be searching for a second wind. You may also be wondering if all this hoopla is worth your investment in time, money, and energy. And the answer is yes. There's a world of opportunity for you to bring real joy to others over the next week.

Because of its mass commercialism, a modern Christmas can be used to actually put Jesus back into the season. The weeks leading up to Christmas, with the constant bombardment of television specials, commercials, and decorations, can become a platform for spreading the true meaning of Christmas. In fact, the way the holiday has evolved over the past fifty years sets the stage for an incredible missionary movement. And you can easily and comfortably be a part of this movement.

A couple centuries ago celebrating Christmas was outlawed in many sections of the United States. In the years just before and after the American Revolution, the holiday was ignored. Most stores and factories stayed open on Christmas—doing business as usual—unless December 25 fell on a Sunday, when stores were closed anyway. Back then no one thought about celebrating Christ's birth until Christmas Eve. Even in the days before World War II, the Christmas holiday did not stretch for weeks. Eighty years ago shopping and the holiday activities orchestrated by churches, schools, and other organizations were all done during the week leading up to Christmas.

For centuries churches felt they had the handle on Christmas. They dictated the way the holiday would be celebrated. After stores took charge, many Christians felt left out as they saw that lights of the season marked holiday sales more than the babe in the manger. From pulpits, preachers declared that Christmas was no longer a religious holiday. They lamented that commercialization had turned Christ's birthday into a secular orgy of spending. Yet those who looked beyond newspaper sales circulars and mail-order catalogs saw something spiritual at work. The first clear signs of this new Christmas could be seen overseas.

During World War II, thanks to a president extending the holiday season, American military personnel organized Christmas celebrations in places that had never heard of the holiday. Unknowingly, these men and women exported Christmas traditions and songs to the far corners of the world. Just by singing carols like "O Holy Night," "Silent Night," and "Joy to the World" and reading from the gospel of Luke and opening gifts, these Americans were living out the final challenge Christ gave to his disciples: "Go and make disciples of all nations, baptizing them in the name of the Father and of the Son and of the Holy Spirit, and teaching them to obey everything I have commanded you" (Matt. 28:19–20).

Foreigners observed the American GIs and saw the joy that celebrating Christmas brought to men and women caught in the middle of a horrible war. If this day was so special that it could bring smiles in the midst of war's unholy terror, they wanted to join in the celebration too. The GIs had planted the holiday season in areas that had long been thought of as barren ground for missionaries.

After the war, in places where American troops had been stationed, children who had never heard of Jesus before were drawing manger scenes and making wish lists. Santa Claus began to appear on Christmas Eve. Christmas was becoming a holiday all around the globe. Santa Claus and commercialism had not ruined Christmas; just the opposite had happened. The focus on the holiday opened up a huge door of opportunity to tell the real story — the birth of Jesus.

This hit home in my world when my book *Stories Behind the Great Traditions of Christmas* was translated into Chinese. Who would have thought that folks in the Orient would want to know the stories behind things like holly, ivy, Advent, and Christmas trees? Yet in the same way that the American military sowed seeds during World War II, cable news stations are now sowing them by broadcasting stories about the holidays all over the globe, and the internet is sowing them by pumping out Christmas features and email forwards. The commercialization of the holiday is helping make it more widely known and accepted.

Christmas is almost everywhere. This gives us a chance to talk about the real meaning of the season with those who have never set foot in a church. We now have a platform to get the word out about Jesus, to tell the true story of Christmas. This is an opportunity we shouldn't ignore.

Remember, Christ used weddings and feasts to spread God's message. We can do the same. We can be sensitive for opportunities to spread the word while shopping, doing charity work, giving out presents. Through our actions, we can use commercialism to put Jesus back in the season. And we don't even have to leave our hometowns.

This year spread the word with Bible verses. When you wrap your gifts, write the reference to your favorite Bible verse on the tag. When you send out greeting cards, put a Scripture reference on your return address—something like John 3:16 ("God so loved the world ...") or Matthew 25:35–40 ("I was hungry and you gave me something to eat ...") or maybe, since this is the season of love, 1 Corinthians 13:13 ("Now these three remain: faith, hope and love. But the greatest of these is love.")

Whatever is your favorite verse, write the reference to it below your name and address or on the envelope flap. Some folks will look that verse up, and who knows where that will lead? Try leaving the Bible in your home open to the second chapter of Luke. These small actions can quietly have a huge impact. By showing your joy, as the GIs did in World War II, you lead others to want to find out more about the story behind the holiday.

One of the keys to being a part of this missionary movement is knowing why we do what we do at Christmas. Spend some time learning what our traditions mean. Learn the story of poinsettias so you can tell others about the spiritual symbols. Know that in using holly and ivy, the green represents everlasting life and the red was the color early Christians connected to Christ's blood. Knowing the symbolism can open a spiritual dialog.

Many people get angry when they see the word *Christmas* written as *Xmas*, without *Christ* spelled out. Yet for more than a thousand years the church wrote it this way. Why? In the Ancient Greek language, the large *X* was the first letter in the word *Christ*. So *Xmas* actually meant "worshiping Christ."

Early Christians used to make an *X* to show they were men and women of faith. Many even placed an *X* over the door of their homes. Sometimes when a Christian died defending the faith, other believers marked the letter *X* on the ground where that person fell. By knowing the stories behind using the word *Xmas* to refer to Christmas, you can put Jesus out front and tell the real meaning of his time on earth.

In the next week, watch for a situation in which you can subtly tell someone about the meaning of the season. The fact that almost everyone celebrates Christmas in one way or another gives you that chance. We complain about the commercialization of Christmas, not realizing that it opens the door for us to share the good news. Take advantage of this opportunity. Spread the real joy of Christmas and, in the process, live out Christ's final charge to his disciples.

A Shortcut to the Spirit of the Season

To spread the holy part of the holiday, invite your friends and family to a church service or choir concert, where they will hear the message of the first Christmas. All you risk in extending this invitation is a "No, thanks." Yet when someone does attend, you have helped to give them an understanding of the true meaning of Christmas.

DAY 19

PRESERVING THE HOLIDAYS

The holidays can be a trying time. We are involved in activities that seem to have little value. Presents we carefully wrap are hastily ripped open to find what is inside. Decorations are put up only to be taken down a few weeks later. People come and go so fast, we barely realize they were there. We spend hours preparing grand meals, then more hours trying to get rid of leftovers. The time, money, and effort we invest in the holidays often seem to have been spent unwisely. Everything at Christmas seems transitory and void of any real deep and lasting value.

We need to get back to the true meaning of Christmas. We must revisit our memories to put into perspective the value of the season and all the things we do to make it special. Record those memories. Write them down. Dig out the old photos. Preserving and presenting those vital moments of Christmas past can be one of the best presents you will give your family.

In 1941, right after the attack on Pearl Harbor and the start of World War II, Bing Crosby introduced on his national radio program a song that would become the best-selling Christmas recording of all time. In almost all the versions of "White Christmas" recorded and played today, Irving Berlin's original introduction is deleted. Written for the movie *Holiday Inn*, the song's now almost forgotten opening lyrics told of a person spending the holidays alone in Beverly Hills, California. The weather was warm, the skies were clear, and the sun was shining, but as beautiful and ideal as the day seemed, the singer longed for the Christmases of his past when it was crisp, cold, and snowy.

Three years later singer-songwriter Mel Torme was suffering through a hot July. He was supposed to be composing music for a big-budget Hollywood musical, but the heat had zapped his energy and, in the process, created an inspirational drought. Sitting down at the piano and playing with the keys, Torme glanced at a notebook containing that day's scribbling of close friend and songwriting partner Robert Wells. It seemed that in an effort to bring a hint of cool air to the furnace-like environment, Wells had begun to write down his memories of Christmases in New England. As he played on the piano, Torme verbally added his own special recollections. Soon the day not only seemed much cooler, but memories of holidays past, when Jack Frost nipped at noses and chestnuts were sold on city street corners, were combined into a holiday treasure known as "The Christmas Song."

Like Irving Berlin, Mel Torme, and Robert Wells, we all have special memories of past holidays. Yet while these composers shared their reminiscences in lyrical form, giving us special musical treats, we allow our memories to remain in the far recesses of our minds and in attic boxes. What we fail to understand is that our memories have power. When recalled in detail, they can transform a moment and bring back to life the special people and memories from our past.

We need to create our own versions of "White Christmas" and "The Christmas Song." In fact, doing that will help us get the most out of this year's celebrations. You don't have to be a composer to create a personal Christmas carol. But first you must return to the past.

In the famous novel that has been spun into a number of motion pictures, Charles Dickens takes Scrooge back into the past to revisit the holidays of his youth. The sour old man rediscovers many of the sweetest moments of his life. Over time he comes to see the world of his past life standing in stark contrast to the world he now calls home. In the end, he changes his attitude in order to embrace the full joy of the holiday season.

Most of us don't walk through the holiday as Scrooge did in *A Christmas Carol.* We don't hate the holiday or wish it would go away. Yet at times we all get overwhelmed by the demands of the season. As the final hours to another Christmas wind down, it is worth taking a trip with a ghost of Christmas past. In fact, it should be required for everyone before the holiday.

In my own life, there are a handful of Christmas memories that stand out from all the rest. There was the night I got the electric train. (We always opened our gifts on Christmas Eve.) And another when I received my first transistor radio. I vividly remember the magic of those years. I recall my feelings, the way the room looked, and even the chill in the air. Through the years, those moments have remained crystal clear.

At first your time travel will initiate memories of a jumble of events all strung together in soft focus. Don't quit. Keep concentrating on those special days of yore, and a few images will emerge. As your vision clears, you will see events unfold as if they were happening now. You'll feel younger and maybe more innocent. Spend a few minutes in your memory and notice the sense of joy and awe that swirls around you like the snowflakes Bing dreamed of in "White Christmas." You'll hear the sounds of that day as clearly as Mel Torme recalled the Yuletide carols. Memories will flow over you like a wave and take you to a place where time stands still. Suddenly the joy of the season will be alive, and the carol locked in your mind will be your own.

As you really focus, your memory will revolve around a

specific toy, activity, or meal. When you find it, lock on to that moment and allow yourself to become fully immersed in it. Reliving the moment is just the beginning. When you have captured those memories, it is time to take the next step.

Start this year to write down your best Christmas experiences. Then, when you have fully recorded your story on paper, put it somewhere safe. But don't hide it; place it where others can read it. A scrapbook with photos taken when that memory was created is ideal. Add to your scrapbook every Christmas. Include more stories, more photos, and even recipes, a piece of wrapping paper from a special present. In time this book will become a treasured item that everyone in the family will want to look through — a tie that connects your Christmases and makes each one alive again.

The computer is a great way to not only write your stories but also share them. Send a story via email to others who were a part of a special celebration. You might just invigorate a memory for them as well.

Earlier in this book, we looked at the angel in the beloved Frank Capra film *It's a Wonderful Life.* The heavenly visitor, Clarence, essentially took George into the past to help him gain a much deeper understanding of his life. When the savings and loan director relived those old times, he was transformed from a hopeless failure to a blessed and successful man. Writing down your best holiday memories can give you a better perspective on Christmas and on your life, just as it did for George. If you are feeling down, you can be lifted up. If you are tired, a memory can rejuvenate you. If you are mired in hopelessness, you might even find the light that leads you to a brighter place.

Writing down and reliving your best holidays can connect you with a new generation. Although the popular gifts change from year to year, and things you wanted as a child become antiques, the emotions don't change; they're just like the emotions you had. By reading your memories and looking at the photos in your special holiday scrapbook, your children and grandchildren will travel a bridge that connects the generations. Your written record has the power to bring back past Christmases again and again, even long after you are no longer walking this earth.

We are the sum of our memories. Memories put life into perspective. They inspire us. Don't let them slip away. Write them down and create a legacy that will help light the holidays for years to come.

~~~~~~~~~~

A Shortcut to the Spirit of the Season

Complete scrapbook kits are available in hobby stores, craft stores, and office supply stores. Free websites, such as www.scrapbooking.com and www .scrapbook.com, can help you get started. Creating a scrapbook is easy and will be a permanent record for future generations.

BEGINNING TO DISCOVER PEACE ON EARTH

In his classic song "Here Comes Santa Claus," Gene Autry penned a couple lines that added a spiritual quality to the fanciful children's classic: "Peace on earth will come to all / If we just follow the light." This message is not just in the singing cowboy's first holiday hit song but also in sermons, in newspapers columns, in speeches, and on cards. "Peace on earth, goodwill to men" — these words were spoken at the first Christmas.

We hear the words, but how many of us really pursue "goodwill to men"? The question to be asked is, do you really wish goodwill for all those you know, or are you still seeking to settle old scores and hold on to unimportant grudges? Peace comes with a price grounded in humility. To have peace in your holidays, put goodwill into action.

Jesus spoke of peace, kindness, and love. His messages evoked themes of forgiveness and service. While thousands came to hear him speak, many who heard Jesus' words were surely confused by his tone. They had prayed for a Messiah who would take up the sword and vanquish God's enemies. A peace beyond the world's understanding was not on their wish list. They wanted a peace that could come only after every foe had been killed.

Personal peace is a reflection of what is hidden in the heart. You can see personal peace in the eyes, the touch, and the actions. Those who have truly found this spiritual serenity don't sweat the small stuff. They don't focus on what has been done to them; instead they focus on what they can do for others. To have true peace on your piece of the earth, the best place to begin is by looking inward.

Few are aware of it as they frown and fret during the holidays. In my own family, I have seen misunderstandings and old feuds cause incredible tension at Christmas gatherings. Even if no words were spoken and past spats were not mentioned, the anger and hurt that seeped from hearts caused such a dark cloud to settle over the entire proceedings that even the children could feel it. I have found that in most family disputes, pride is what makes the holidays stormy.

Begin the process of finding your peace on earth. While

it might be humbling, it is not really that difficult. The last thing any of us should be is the person who disrupts the peace. If a family war is raging in your life, find the cause and, with a Christian compassion, try to resolve the conflict.

Most conflicts begin with poorly chosen words. One of the sad facts in life is that there is no way to grab spoken words out of the air and stuff them back into our mouths. Once we say something, the damage is done. Like an untreated wound, these words keep inflicting pain for a long time. They can even kill a relationship.

The other major cause of conflict is an ill-conceived action. Overcome by everything from enthusiasm to greed, people often act without thinking of the consequences.

If your words or actions have created conflicts in life, start the healing process by speaking two well-known words. The shortest sentence that can transform almost any situation and bring peace is "I'm sorry." The question becomes, can you bring yourself to say those words?

If you can humble yourself and admit your mistakes, you are on your way to becoming a peacemaker. Even before you pick up the phone or walk out your door to seek out that old friend or family member, look in the mirror. Start your journey to peace by forgiving yourself for past wrongs and foolish mistakes.

In John 14:27, Jesus told those closest to him, "Peace I leave with you; my peace I give you. I do not give to you as the world gives. Do not let your hearts be troubled and do not be afraid."

Give your burden to God. After you surrender what is troubling your heart and filling your head, you will probably find ways to lift others caught in the same trap.

The story behind one special holiday carol might just provide a road map for what can be accomplished when you focus on the positive. More than six decades ago Jill Jackson was lost in darkness. Countless times she had been kicked and abused by her own family. Only after she had suffered incredible spiritual anguish was the little girl turned over to the state. After that she spent much of her young life living in orphanages and feeling unwanted. When she was a young adult, a promising career in motion pictures was shattered by a bad marriage that brought back the memories of being rejected by her parents. Left alone with a small child, overwhelmed by bills and responsibilities, the woman who had never known real love attempted to take her own life.

Jackson survived, but her actions left her partially paralyzed. Lost, adrift, and alone, she studied each of the world's major religions in an effort to find some kind of self-esteem. Like many wandering and confused souls, she even dipped into New Age thoughts. She finally found the answers she needed in the words and teachings of Christ. After throwing away the false behavior of trying to control things she couldn't, as well as her guilt at trying to end her own life, she gained a new perspective. With peace in her heart, she saw her full potential and became immersed in a river of joy. In 1955, with the help of her second husband, Jackson composed a song that reflected the wisdom she had gained through her faith.

"Let There Be Peace on Earth" became a huge hit in the early 1960s. For many, Jackson's personal testimony was an anthem that offered hope in an era filled with violence and war. Yet even as the song was performed in churches, on concert stages, and at rallies to protest war, many missed the key element of faith that was so clear in both Jackson's lyrics and the life of Jesus. For the world to have true peace, peace has to be rooted inside each human heart.

Can you imagine the horror Jill Jackson felt over attempting to end her own life? She had to move past that moment and forgive herself to seek answers and find her potential. Once she did, she found the peace Christ spoke of to his disciples. And she became a light in the world.

Christmas should remind us that it is never too late for a second chance. Forgive yourself for past unwise and irresponsible actions. Keep the words of "Let There Be Peace on Earth" in your mind as you begin your quest for peace.

Your next step is to make a list of the people you have hurt. Contact each one and apologize for what you did. When you say you are sorry, don't add "but." Instead go beyond just the apology and explain why you want to build a bridge of understanding with the other person. Point out the things that make him or her important to you. While careless words create voids, carefully chosen words build strong bridges. Lift the other person with your words.

Those you reach out to may not accept your efforts. Even then, it is important to remember that you tried to bring peace to a situation. Being the first to move in the direction of reconciliation isn't a sign of weakness; it's a sign of strength. Christmas is a good time to begin the process.

Finally, in your quest for peace, it's important how you present yourself to others. As you run errands, shop, or go to special events, you come into contact with a lot of people. If peace on earth is to begin with you, you need to be positive along every step of your path. Reach out in kindness. Use a smile to light your way. Lift others up with your tone of voice and your words. A compliment or a simple thank-you might well bring peace to someone's life. Make the world of others a kinder place, and yours will be more peaceful as well.

Remember that peace begins when a person feels safe, secure, and wanted. People will be coming to your home over the next few days. Make your home that refuge of peace. Let your face glow with holiday cheer when you greet your guests. Reach out with a warm touch. Make them feel that by just being there, they are making your Christmas much more special. Show your enthusiasm from the moment you see them, and they will feel they have found holiday joy and peace.

Jesus spoke often of peace, but nothing he said defines

the rewards of being a peacemaker better than his words in Matthew 5:9: "Blessed are the peacemakers, for they will be called children of God."

Christ came to earth so that we can find peace in our hearts even as the world recklessly rushes down paths of destruction. Start the simple practice of forgiving and accepting yourself. Apologize to those you have hurt. And make your world a refuge of love, warmth, and security. Do all this, and you will surely find peace on earth.

~~~~~~~~~~

A Shortcut to the Spirit of the Season

In Luke 2:14 we find these words: "Glory to God in the highest, and on earth peace, good will toward men" (KJV). Live by the words of this simple verse. Stop judging; reach out in gentle kindness; follow the teachings of Christ. When you feel anger or impatience, just whisper the words in this verse, and they will help return peace to your world.

DAY 21

HOOKING YOURSELF
TO AN OLD TRADITION

Years ago when Gene Autry recorded "Rudolph the Red-Nosed Reindeer," he also cut a song called "If It Doesn't Snow on Christmas." The main worry for many kids during the holidays is snow. If there is no snow, how is Santa going to use his sleigh? The lyrics continue this theme as the child wishes the jolly old elf could fly a plane, take a train, or use a bus. And beyond the concerns about snow, we have all heard the questions "How will Santa find us?" "But we don't have a chimney! How will he get in?" "Are you sure Santa knows we're at Grandma's?"

Christmas can be even more overwhelming for children

than it is for adults. It's an exciting and demanding time. Normal routines vanish. There is so much to see, so many choices, presents to think about, programs at school and church to participate in, parties to attend. And there's that visit from St. Nick to fret about.

Perhaps the toughest task people face during the holiday season is finding and maintaining focus. During these demanding days, vision is fragmented, thoughts are scattered, and systems are on overload. Many people are simply overwhelmed by having to accomplish so much in the short number of days left before Christmas. As the clock ticks down, stress levels go up. Some folks are so overcome with duties, they cannot wait to get everything about the holidays behind them.

One of the simplest tools that can put Jesus back on the holiday map is also one of the season's most loved treats. It is low-cost, easy to find, and opens at least one door that can lead to a much more spiritual holiday.

Many of our holiday traditions are based on symbolism. The early church took well-known customs and transformed them into Christian teaching tools. Though its tie to the season is not nearly as old as that of most traditions, a confectioner's creation has a history of putting the focus of Christmas back on Christ. A simple way to keep Jesus front and center during your holidays and to fully explain your faith is as near as a box of candy canes.

Hard candy is one of the world's oldest treats. Thousands

of years ago children were begging their parents for the tasty delight. Because the real St. Nicholas often gave candy to children, candy has been associated with Christmas for at least seventeen hundred years. In 1670 a choirmaster in Germany found a way to use the sweet treat as a tool to keep children focused on the real story of the holiday.

He noticed that during lengthy church services, kids would get bored and begin to act out. Whispers were heard, and more than a few children had their hair pulled. There were tears. Because the Christmas worship services were so long, it seemed that the worst conduct usually occurred then.

After years of employing threats and even giving spankings to those who misbehaved during the holiday festivities, the choirmaster finally turned to what many in his congregation saw as bribery. He had a candy maker bend the white sticks of hard candy into the shape of a shepherd's staff. The choirmaster chose this type of confectionary treat because it would take the children a long time to eat it. He reasoned that the longer they licked their candy sticks, the quieter they would be.

Knowing that many did not approve of his tactics, the director felt a need to create a holiday lesson to justify his actions. Before the service, as he handed out the candy to the excited children, he explained that the color white represented the purity of Christ. Showing them the unique shape, he said the candy had been molded in this way to represent a shepherd's staff, to remind them of the sheepherders' role in the first Christmas. He ended his lesson by explaining that the shape should also remind the children of Jesus, as he was known as the Good Shepherd. Thus began the candy cane's association with the Christian faith.

What started in Germany as a way to keep children quiet quickly became a tasty Christmas decoration. Within a hundred years white candy canes were being placed on Christmas trees throughout Eastern Europe. Prince Albert brought the custom to England when he married Queen Victoria. The candy continued its global trek when it was added to American Christmas tree decorations in the years after the Civil War.

The lessons first taught by the choirmaster are a good reason to add this treat to your holiday decorations, as they contain a trio of the central points of Christmas history. These points are timeless, and the lessons are still powerful for both young and old. Yet thanks to two Americans, another twist has been added that makes the candy cane a more dramatic teaching and witnessing tool.

In the 1920s candy maker Bob McCormick had a shop in Albany, Georgia. After years of experimenting, the confectioner found a way to hand twist colors into the candy canes. Once he placed them on the market, sales of his colorful hard candy sticks quickly outpaced those of the traditional white ones.

Using this new method, an Indiana candy maker added three red stripes to his formerly solid white canes. He told those who worked for him that the three stripes represented the Trinity and that the red color stood for the blood Jesus shed for all humankind. Just as the choirmaster had so many years before, the man further explained that the white represented purity and that the crook symbolized the staff of a shepherd. The candy maker then turned the cane upside down and pointed out that it was now the letter *J*, as a reminder of the babe in the manger who would give his life for the world's sins. As the Indiana confectioner's story spread, churches began to hand out the red-striped treats to children. Kids ate them, and teachers retold the symbolic story of colors and shapes.

You too can use the candy cane in a variety of ways as you embrace its tie to the holiday. Like the Germans did three centuries ago, you can hang it on your tree. You can also hand out candy canes as treats. They are great stocking stuffers, can be used as decorations on cakes, and can even be combined with the bows you place on your presents.

If you have a computer, create and print a small piece of paper that tells the story behind the symbolism found in the candy cane. Then tie a story to each cane you hang up or hand out. This simple act will draw others' attention back to the reasons why God sent his Son to earth.

This connection between the candy cane and the story of Jesus is one children will never forget. It's a lesson they'll pass along to friends. Years later, when the kids grow up and see a candy cane, they will no doubt think back to a particular Christmas in childhood and remember the first time they heard the story of the candy cane.

The simple candy cane opens doors for witnessing, for telling others about Jesus. Yet beyond being a tool for reaching others, the candy cane can help you refocus your vision on the joy, the wonder, and the impact of the events that happened in a stable so long ago.

~~~~~~~~~~

A Shortcut to the Spirit of the Season

Put a candy cane in your purse or coat pocket as a reminder to keep your eye on Christ during this time of year when the world celebrates his birth. With that singular focus, you will have a much more meaningful holiday season.

Day 22

Cooking Up the Spirit of Christmas

One of the oldest traditions of Christmas is the preparation of food—a gift for the senses. There is nothing like the smell of something special baking in the kitchen to make the holiday suddenly come alive. The familiar aromas not only warm hearts but also bring smiles as everyone anticipates the taste of the foods that have become family traditions.

Christmas feasts date back about seventeen hundred years to the time when the holiday was first celebrated. The emphasis on food is such a large part of the season that the first Christmas card showed a Victorian family sitting around a table filled with the finest English cuisine.

In our modern age of microwaves, frozen dinners, and eating out, Christmas is one of the few times of the year when almost everyone is motivated to make dinner a special event. Recipes are pulled out of the cupboard, and family favorites are prepared in much the same way Grandma used to do it.

From my perspective, what really tickles and tempts the taste buds are the homemade desserts and candies. I still remember clearly from my childhood that everyone seemed to have a specialty dish that was theirs alone. One of my grandmothers prepared the best peanut brittle in the world. My other grandmother whipped up fudge cookies that everyone searched for from the moment they entered her house. My mother created divinity and cheesecake. My wife is famous for her Christmas cookies. She had a grandmother who scored hits with her homemade popcorn balls. I always chime in with my peanut butter fudge. During Christmas, there are so many different choices and so little room on the plate. It seems you can't go anywhere without someone offering you a treat.

Think back to the loved ones in your life and the special goodies they cooked up over the holidays. Rework that magic. Bring some of those old cherished memories back to life. Make it a team effort. Include as many members of your family as you can in preparing these incredible treats of the season. It doesn't matter if they can cook or not. Just having them with you provides a grand new world of opportunity for joyful family bonding.

The kitchen is the gathering spot in most homes. This is the place where triumphs and tragedies are discussed. It is the heart of your home. Invite others into your domain. Give them a bowl and a spoon and let the fun begin. Family stories will naturally find their way into the conversations. Record those stories. Take pictures. Capture those moments of laughter and smiles as you share memories.

And don't worry about the mess. This is a time for communion and reunion. Have fun. Laugh over any spilled milk. Relax. When it's time to decorate the goodies, let the kids (and the grown-ups) go wild with colors and sprinkles. Create an atmosphere that lifts spirits and produces deep bonds. You might even hum a few bars from the old hymn "Blest Be the Tie That Binds" and get everyone to join in. Have the person who plays a guitar strum along. Preparing holiday treats in the warmth of your kitchen can become a tie that does bind the generations of your family together.

The holiday baking task that entertains both children and adults is making Christmas cookies. Easy favorites are reindeer, holly, bells, snowmen, and ornaments. The myriad of icing colors and the wide variety of ways there are to add finishing touches can be both challenging and fun. As artistic instincts take over, this kitchen exercise provides some of the season's best moments for photos. So have your camera ready and don't miss anything, from the joy on a child's face as he or she spreads icing on a cookie to tiny hands dusty with flour, or a smudge of flour on a nose. Capture the over-all scene. Get close-ups.

If you've never made Christmas cookies before, let me help. You can buy cookie cutters at almost any store — variety, grocery, discount, kitchen outlet, and even antique stores. A good recipe for these goodies was created by one of our family friends. It's one of the easiest and best known to humanity.

Brenda McGregor's Christmas Cookies

Put 1 cup of butter, 2 eggs, 1½ cups of sugar, and 3 teaspoons of vanilla in a bowl and stir into a creamy mixture.

In a second bowl, place 3½ cups of flour, ½ teaspoon of salt, and 2½ teaspoons of baking powder. Blend to-gether and then add to creamy mixture.

Roll combined ingredients into a large ball and chill. When chilled, roll the mixture out with a rolling pin and cut into shapes with cookie cutters. Place cookies on a baking sheet and put them into an oven that has been preheated to 350° F. Bake until they just begin to turn light brown.

Icing: 2 cups of powdered sugar, 1 tablespoon of but-ter, 3 tablespoons of milk, 1 teaspoon of vanilla, ¼ tea-spoon of salt, and food coloring as needed.

Spread icing on the cookies right after they come out of the oven.

You don't have to begin and end with cookies. You can make sausage balls.

Sausage Balls

Mix together in a bowl a pound of grated cheese, a pound of ground sausage, and a cup of flour. Form into marble-sized balls and bake on an ungreased cookie sheet at 350° F. for ten minutes or until the balls have taken on a hint of brown.

And nothing is easier than peanut butter fudge. This holiday treat can be made in a microwave.

Peanut Butter Fudge

Ingredients: 1 cup of butter, 1 cup of peanut butter, 1 teaspoon of vanilla, and 1 pound of powdered sugar.

Microwave butter and peanut butter for two minutes on high. Now that they have been softened by the heat, stir them together and microwave on high for two more minutes. Add vanilla and powdered sugar to peanut butter mixture and stir with a wooden spoon. Pour into a buttered 8-by-8-inch pan lined with waxed paper. Place a second piece of waxed paper on the surface of the fudge and refrigerate until cool. Cut into pieces.

My grandmothers taught me a very important Christmas lesson. They didn't just bake treats for their families; they shared their goodies with others. Too often sharing gets lost, even at Christmas. During this season, put the focus back on sharing. Sharing what you make shines a bright light in the direction of giving and teaches that lesson to your children ... and grandchildren.

Read to them the message of Matthew 25:34–40:

> The King will say to those on his right, "Come, you who are blessed by my Father; take your inheritance, the kingdom prepared for you since the creation of the world. For I was hungry and you gave me something to eat, I was thirsty and you gave me something to drink, I was a stranger and you invited me in, I needed clothes and you clothed me, I was sick and you looked after me, I was in prison and you came to visit me."
>
> Then the righteous will answer him, "Lord, when did we see you hungry and feed you, or thirsty and give you something to drink? When did we see you a stranger and invite you in, or needing clothes and clothe you? When did we see you sick or in prison and go to visit you?"
>
> The King will reply, "Truly I tell you, whatever you did for one of the least of these brothers and sisters of mine, you did for me."

Explain to your children and grandchildren what these

words mean and why what Jesus said here is so important. To make sure these verses take root, connect them with all the special holiday drives — the Santas ringing bells outside stores, the angel trees at malls — that give to those who have little or nothing. What each of us needs to focus on as an annual tradition of Christmas is giving to "the least of these." You might even teach the lesson of tithing as you help your kids and grandkids select a portion of the treats they created to give away to those who have so little. Have them fill special plates with the goodies they prepared with their own hands. Then take the children with you as you deliver the treats to the people they otherwise would never meet. As you make your rounds, remind the kids of the gifts the wise men brought Jesus.

Finally, before you hand out any of your cookies and candies, explain to your children that Jesus, the babe in the manger, was God's special gift to each of us, that God loves us all. Let them know that by giving part of what they made with their labor, they are sharing God's gift of love. Tell them that giving is essential to both Christmas and faith.

As you arrive at your delivery stops, make the kids a part of the giving. Introduce them. Have them give the plates of goodies and describe what they made. Children, by sharing with others, learn that they are making a difference in someone's life. They are showing, with their gifts, that they love and appreciate those who might otherwise be forgotten. In reaching out to "the least of these," they are acting as Christ would.

By including your children and grandchildren in this holiday experience of giving, you pass along this wonderful Christmas tradition. You make it an important part of family giving. Great lessons come through combining talents and faith.

I've emphasized teaching the lessons of giving to kids and grandkids. That's how I learned them, from my grandmothers. But these same lessons can be passed on even if you can't include others in preparing and delivering the goodies. Head to the kitchen anyway. As you work, focus on the joy you have in what you're doing. Then give to others a tithe of what you make. On your rounds, as you hand out the goodies, you are letting others know that you're thinking of them, that they haven't been forgotten. And notice the response you receive as you deliver your special brand of family warmth, love, and kindness. Especially the smiles.

~~~~~~~~~~~~~~~

A Shortcut to the Spirit of the Season

Start a new holiday tradition by adding a new recipe, one that will be on the request list year after year. A host of ideas can be found in current magazines. Go online and search for Christmas recipes. To cut down on the number of results, type the names of specific treats in the search engine, such as "peanut brittle" or "cinnamon rolls." Or try a new recipe for stuffing for the turkey.

DAY 23

REFLECTING ON THE PAST

It's the eve of Christmas Eve. You probably have most of your shopping completed, gifts wrapped, and the house in order. If your house is like ours, things will be hectic tomorrow. Build in time for a pause and a break before the next two big days.

One of the best ways to relax and keep life in perspective is to count your blessings. We all have a myriad of things for which we are thankful. At Christmas, maybe the best place to begin counting your blessings is by thanking God for the gift of his Son.

Christmas is the most wonderful time of the year because it celebrates the most important event that ever happened on this planet. So as you begin counting your blessings, forget about all the money you spent, the work you did, and the time it took to make this holiday special at your house. Instead rejoice in the fact that everything you did was worth it because Christmas needs to be remembered, embraced, enjoyed, and treasured. As a Christian, you are a standard bearer of the wonder of this season. You open the door to the joy of the holiday to all those who come into your world. In that way, you are like the angels who came to visit the shepherds.

After you have counted your blessings and reaffirmed the world's need for Christmas, open your Bible and, in Matthew and Luke, read the short passages of Scripture that tell about the birth of Christ. These verses have inspired countless songs, books, movies, and art. Their power is so great, they have stopped wars. In fact, the first words ever spoken over the air in a radio broadcast were taken from the second chapter of Luke.

Turn back the clock to 1906, to Christmas Eve. Imagine for a moment you are listening to a small speaker clicking out messages in Morse code. Then, from out of nowhere, the audible dots and dashes are interrupted by a man's voice. You are hearing what the world believes is impossible! The human voice is being transmitted through the air, by means of radio waves. You are riveted in your chair, shocked beyond reason, and then you realize the speaker is broadcasting the words found in the first thirty-two verses of Luke 2. Imagine the impact these words would have had on you that night!

Now read Luke 2 aloud, as if you were hearing these words for the first time. As you again take in the Christmas story, consider the joy of the angels, the wonder of the shepherds, and the pride of Mary and Joseph.

> In those days Caesar Augustus issued a decree that a census should be taken of the entire Roman world. (This was the first census that took place while Quirinius was governor of Syria.) And everyone went to their own town to register.
>
> So Joseph also went up from the town of Nazareth in Galilee to Judea, to Bethlehem the town of David, because he belonged to the house and line of David. He went there to register with Mary, who was pledged to be married to him and was expecting a child. While they were there, the time came for the baby to be born, and she gave birth to her firstborn, a son. She wrapped him in cloths and placed him in a manger, because there was no guest room available for them.
>
> And there were shepherds living out in the fields nearby, keeping watch over their flocks at night. An angel of the Lord appeared to them, and the glory of the Lord shone around them, and they were terrified. But the angel said to them, "Do not be afraid. I bring you good news of great joy that will be for all the people. Today in the town of David a Savior has been born to you; he is the Messiah, the Lord. This will be a sign to

you: You will find a baby wrapped in cloths and lying in a manger."

Suddenly a great company of the heavenly host appeared with the angel, praising God and saying,

"Glory to God in the highest heaven,
    and on earth peace to those on whom his favor rests."

When the angels had left them and gone into heaven, the shepherds said to one another, "Let's go to Bethlehem and see this thing that has happened, which the Lord has told us about."

So they hurried off and found Mary and Joseph, and the baby, who was lying in the manger. When they had seen him, they spread the word concerning what had been told them about this child, and all who heard it were amazed at what the shepherds said to them. But Mary treasured up all these things and pondered them in her heart. The shepherds returned, glorifying and praising God for all the things they had heard and seen, which were just as they had been told.

On the eighth day, when it was time to circumcise the child, he was named Jesus, the name the angel had given him before he was conceived.

When the time came for the purification rites required by the Law of Moses, Joseph and Mary took him to Jerusalem to present him to the Lord (as it is written in the Law of the Lord, "Every firstborn male is to be consecrated to the Lord"), and to offer a sacrifice in keeping with what is said in the Law of the Lord: "a pair of doves or two young pigeons."

Now there was a man in Jerusalem called Simeon, who was righteous and devout. He was waiting for the consolation of Israel, and the Holy Spirit was on him. It had been revealed to him by the Holy Spirit that he would not die before he had seen the Lord's Messiah. Moved by the Spirit, he went into the temple courts. When the parents brought in the child Jesus to do for him what the custom of the Law required, Simeon took him in his arms and praised God, saying:

"Sovereign Lord, as you have promised,
    you may now dismiss your servant in peace.
For my eyes have seen your salvation,
    which you have prepared in the sight of all nations:
a light for revelation to the Gentiles,
    and the glory of your people Israel."

Luke 2:1–32

Now, as you remember the shepherds and the wise men who traveled to see the baby Jesus, think of those you know who will be traveling this Christmas. These travelers need to be watched over just as were those whose journeys made the first Christmas complete. Remember that what makes this holiday special, even more than the decorations and songs, is people coming together. Take a moment and say a prayer for the travelers.

This is a season to smile, to laugh, and even sometimes to cry. Great movies from Christmas past can touch our deepest emotions. Remember the joy you felt the first time you saw a treasured classic holiday film. Relive that experience. Gather family members around to watch *It's a Wonderful Life*, *Holiday Inn*, *Miracle on 34th Street*, *Christmas in Connecticut*, *An American Christmas Carol*, *The Santa Clause*, or even *Ernest Saves Christmas*. A good movie can whisk you away from the rush of the season and give you time to dwell on what Christmas means, time to get your emotions primed for the next two days.

Christmas cards are another way to get in touch with the meaning of Christmas. Look through the cards you have received. Think of those who took the time to send greetings to you. Seeing their names and reading the notes penned tell you that these people care about you. And they made a special effort to let you know — because of Christmas! Relish these quiet moments. Give yourself time to recharge. Allow all the love and joy of this season to take root in your heart. Let those Christmas emotions push out all the negatives. Remember the words of the angel: "I bring you good tidings of great joy" (Luke 2:10 KJV).

Spread those good tidings to everyone in your world, with that same kind of joy and excitement.

~~~~~~~~~~

A Shortcut to the Spirit of the Season

Step back into Christmas past, to a special song or a TV show, via the internet. A Google search or a site such as YouTube can give you a free trip back to relive special moments. Search for a specific date in history and relive the news of that day. Rediscover the entertainment that was a part of a specific holiday season in the past. The internet can bring old memories into sharp focus and enhance the spirit of the season in a special and personal way.

MAKING THE EXCHANGE OF GIFTS MORE MEANINGFUL

Are you going to miss Christmas? That might seem a strange question to ask on Christmas Eve. After all, Christmas is tomorrow. You're ready. You can't miss it.

Or can you? Can you be so overwhelmed by all the activity on Christmas Day that when it's all over, when you stop to look back on the day, you find that you missed much of what happened?

I'm frustrated by some of the photographs I've taken over the years. In some cases I had the settings on the camera wrong, and the shots I took were either too dark, too light, or out of focus. When I look at these images, I almost have to imagine what happened. On the day after Christmas, when you look back at the last two days, you may find that your mental images seem a lot like those bad photos. The days are nothing more than a blur. Everything that happened is slightly out of focus or missing. The sights, sounds, and smells have been lost forever.

In life, we record our history in our head. These images aren't lasting unless we make them last. Reset your mental camera so you don't miss any of these experiences. Savor these special moments. Like Mary, treasure them in your heart (Luke 2:19).

Stress robs us of these Norman Rockwell elements of Christmas. Many are so concerned that something will not go as planned that they fail to look at all the things that are going right and all the opportunities to relish what is there in front of their eyes. Many have thought about this day for weeks, even months. Many have the ideal Christmas locked in their heads. But they can't relax and enjoy it because they just know something is going to go wrong. Is this you? Then take a trip back in time to view a man so stressed over something he could not control that he couldn't see a solution. Notice the way things worked out when he gave up his plans for spectacular and perfect.

About two centuries ago a young priest carefully placed everything in order for his first Christmas Eve service. The sanctuary looked perfect. After many rehearsals, the choir was in fine form. And he was completely secure in the knowledge that he could deliver his message. Even the weather was cooperating; it was snowy, but not so cold that it would keep people away from the service. Finally it was time. He made his way to his small Austrian church and lit the stove. He walked over to the organ and touched a key. That's when the man was confronted with a crisis. The church's ancient organ would not make a sound. The organ would not even groan. Like many who face a sudden and unexpected problem, this man panicked. Without music, the service would be ruined, and he would look like a poor leader to his flock.

The young priest raced across town to the home of Franz Gruber, a schoolteacher and friend. Gruber listened, then assured Father Moore that everything was going to be all right. He even suggested that the young priest bring his guitar to provide the music.

The words didn't help. Moore was still in a panic. He pointed out that the music he had picked out simply would not work with a guitar. The choir would only be able to do justice to those songs with an organ.

Being a schoolteacher, Gruber understood the need for quick adaptation. Even as his friend frantically paced the room, the older man was sure something could be worked out. To calm Moore down, Gruber suggested that the two of them come up with a song that didn't have a complex arrangement. Surely they could find something. Only then did the priest remember a poem he had written three years before. Still not convinced this would work, he agreed to allow the teacher to set that poem to music.

A few hours later Moore was still worried. He feared that the humble presentation would disappoint his congregation. They were expecting something grand, and all he had was a homemade gift of music. After saying a prayer, he again tried to get the organ going, but it would not budge. The plans he had made were shattered. He expected the worst.

Defeated, the young priest picked up the guitar when it was time for the song. Even though the service had been dramatically altered, the wonder of Christmas was revealed. His worries had been for naught. In fact, on that quiet night, that quickly arranged song made Christmas at the church more powerful and meaningful than it had ever been before.

On that night long ago in Austria, the poem that would have otherwise been left in the bottom of a desk drawer found the light. Today the song which saved that Christmas Eve service is the best-known carol in the world. Can you imagine a Christmas without "Silent Night"?

Father Moore assumed that a broken organ would doom his carefully planned worship service and cause him to appear inadequate in the eyes of his congregation. He was so caught up in failure, he almost missed the spirit of Christmas. In time Moore would come to understand that people can make plans, but God alters them to accomplish something more meaningful.

If Father Moore had thought about the words of Christ, it

might have saved him a lot of worry. Jesus told his disciples not to concern themselves with worldly things but to keep their eyes on God's work. In today's language, Jesus is telling us to forget the little stuff and focus on the whole picture.

Right now the whole picture is Christmas. It's about love, family, and giving. It's about making memories and enjoying each precious moment. It's not about having the perfect tree or an immaculately clean home. And it's definitely not about a note-by-note and line-by-line plan. To enjoy Christmas to the fullest, forget the script. When things get off track, just think of it as creating a road to a new memory.

My wife, Kathy, has the habit of using a theme when she wraps presents. As much as possible, she wraps gifts so that each person has his or her own unique paper. One year, my packages were wrapped in paper that was mainly blue. One of the kids had green and another had red. Kathy's twin sister's presents were wrapped in some kind of plaid pattern. Because my wife knew who had what paper, she didn't bother placing name tags on the packages. As she looked over the perfectly wrapped and arranged presents, she was proud of her carefully constructed plans. What thrilled her most was that none of us knew which gifts were ours. We couldn't pick them up, shake them, and guess what was inside. After years of struggling, she finally had her Christmas under control ... or so she thought.

That year as we began opening our presents, we started to notice strange choices for gifts. Clothes were the wrong size, books were about subjects we usually didn't read about, and the DVDs Kathy picked out didn't match our personalities. Somehow my wife's plan had taken a sharp left turn. Partway through her wrapping, she had mixed up the colors of wrapping paper. Hence our presents were *really* surprises, even to Kathy. She was horrified that she had made such a mistake and tried to figure out how she had gotten so confused. We laughed. Eventually she did too. Far from being some tragedy, the Christmas with the mixed-up wrappings has become one of our family's best holiday memories. Whenever we think back to that night, the memory never fails to bring a smile.

My wife and Father Moore both discovered one of the great rules of Christmas: things are going to go wrong. I doubt that Joseph planned on checking into a stable rather than an inn. Remember the wisdom of Franz Gruber: don't worry or fret. Plans can be adapted. Don't let your mental pictures of the day get out of focus, or you'll miss the heartwarming moments that make these days so special.

Christmas gift-giving can go by in a blur. To bring out the best of what it means to give and receive gifts, try a few of the following suggestions.

Open one present at a time. Put the spotlight on each person who is getting a gift. Give time for the person to enjoy the gift and thank the giver, letting the giver know that what they picked out is something that will be treasured and that their efforts are appreciated. Let everyone see the gift. Then hand out the next gift to someone else.

Christmas Eve was always a huge deal at Grandma's house. Nothing we grandkids received was expensive, but Grandma made sure there were always a lot of presents under the tree. When it came time to tear into them, Grandma always asked one of the smaller kids to hand out the presents. It was a rite of passage to become the official gift giver. Each grandkid recalls that first Christmas Eve when the mantle was passed to him or her. It was part of the family tradition.

As the presents were handed out, we were allowed to set them in front of us but not to open them. We had to wait until everyone had their gifts. Then one person at a time unwrapped a gift. Sometimes there were more than twenty of us in the room and it took forever, but we each saw every present opened, and we each enjoyed the moment when a secret treasure was revealed. And what was most important, we each said thank you to the giver.

One of the things I really loved about Christmas Eve at Grandma's was her lack of concern about how messy things got. By the time we finished opening our presents, wrapping paper covered the floor. I have pictures to prove it. To this day I hate it when folks clean up as they go along. When they start their janitorial work before the presents are all open, it's like leaving a sporting event at halftime. To me, this act of early trash removal proves that these folks are so concerned about organization, they can't relax and take in the wonder of the moment. So one of my cardinal rules for putting on a great Christmas party is to let the paper and ribbon pile up. Don't get in the way. Don't ruin the flow of this special day.

Finally, have the camera ready and take lots of pictures. Document every facet of the celebration. Capture faces as gifts are opened. Take photos both posed and unposed. Get pictures of your family trying clothes on, playing with toys and gadgets, and even watching a movie someone received. Someday one of your kids or grandkids will ask when they got a certain favorite thing, and you can show them a photo of the moment when they unwrapped it.

At the end of the night (if you open presents on Christmas Eve, like we did), when everyone has calmed down and people have gone to bed, look at the mess and smile. The space under the tree might be empty, but so many hearts are now filled with love, and so many minds are overflowing with new memories. Christmas gift giving, whether it went exactly as planned or veered off course, has provided each person with a great sense of security and belonging.

Sit down, relax, and look at the lights on your tree. Think back to that Christmas Eve two hundred years ago in that small church in Austria. Imagine a small choir accompanied by a guitar as, for the first time, they sing "Silent Night." The feelings, the magic, the joy, the power, and the love felt at that Christmas are still alive. Slow down and let the magic of Christmas wash over you.

~~~~~~~~~~~~~~~~~~

A Shortcut to the Spirit of the Season

To make your gift experience more meaningful, write down what everyone received this holiday season. Place the list in your scrapbook or family Bible. This inventory can, years later, bring back a bit of the wonder and love of this Christmas.

DAY 25

SINGING A SPECIAL HAPPY BIRTHDAY

December 25 is one of the most important days on earth. This is the one day that should be filled with more happiness, joy, and wonder than any other day of the year. But by late morning, after all the presents have been opened and the pent-up excitement is over, there's a letdown. It's as if the air has come out of a balloon. In most homes, people are focused on football, playing with new toys, going back to work, or cleaning up the mess. The overriding attitude is boredom. Folks forget the real reason for Christmas.

How will you put Christ back into the season? This question shouldn't have to be asked. Jesus should be the focal point of everything on Christmas Day, not an afterthought. As you think back on all the preparations for Christmas, did anyone think to invite Christ to the party?

You can fix this and stoke a new and brighter holiday fire. It isn't that hard. What day, other than Christmas, do folks get most excited about? The answer is easy. For almost everyone I know, it's a birthday. Why? Birthdays are both meaningful and fun. They are milestones we celebrate, when love flows easily.

Well, Christmas is a birthday too. Perhaps the best way for you to put the spotlight back on Jesus would be to commemorate his birthday in a traditional fashion: with a birthday cake. Invite everyone into the kitchen to bake a cake.

The tradition of having a cake at Christmas goes back hundreds of years and was once one of the most treasured aspects of the holiday. In the Middle Ages, German families would bake a birthday cake for Jesus. In fact, this custom, beyond even gifts, was the one that created the most excitement for children. Back then, cake was a rare treat. Cake meant something special was happening. For Christian families, Christmas was the most important day of the year, so they prepared the best cake. The focus of Christmas was strictly on Christ and family.

The symbolism of the cake meant a great deal and helped to emphasize the lessons of the season. The cakes were white in color, representing the purity of Jesus. If icing was applied, it was red, signifying the blood that Jesus shed for sinners.

The rising of the cake as it baked represented the resurrection of Christ after he died on the cross. A single candle topped the cake, symbolic of the light Christ brought to the world or of the star that the wise men followed. Finally, the cake's sweet taste represented the life awaiting those who accept Jesus as their Savior.

Make baking a cake an integral part of your Christmas celebration. Involve as many family members as you can. Tell the story of the first Christmas as you put the ingredients together. Have different members of your family give the meaning of the various symbols. Have children look in the oven to watch the cake rise.

Shift the focus of Christmas back to the manger, to the birth of Christ, by making Jesus' birthday cake a part of your family's Christmas tradition. When the cake is done and the icing has been added, light the single candle on the cake and lead your family in singing "Happy Birthday" to the one whose birth we celebrate on Christmas Day. At the end of the song, as all eyes are focused on the burning candle, explain that Jesus is the light of the world. Hand a candle to everyone present. Have each person light his or her candle from the single one on the cake. As your family stands in a circle, holding the lit candles, tell them that Jesus is the light that needs to shine through each of them as they go through the next year. You might even sing a chorus of "This Little Light of Mine."

As you share pieces of the cake, start a conversation

about what Jesus needs that we can give him as a gift. As you discuss possible gifts for the babe in the manger, explain the importance of sharing our blessings with others who have less, of telling others the good news of why Jesus came to earth. Some might want to offer their talents to a church group or volunteer for a project or a mission. A few might suggest tithing. Encourage everyone to decide on a personal gift for Jesus and commit to giving it to him in the New Year.

Also, ask for ideas about something everyone can do as a family. Suggest a donation of time to a charity, such as a homeless shelter or food kitchen. Or propose doing something for a needy neighbor or friend, such as painting a house or clearing a yard. Or your family could support an orphaned child through one of the worldwide relief organizations such as World Missionary Evangelism (one of my favorites), Compassion International, or Christian Children's Fund. This might cost each family member a few dollars a month. Such support of a child can create a special bond among family members. Over time, the status of that sponsored child, and what the family's gifts of love have meant, would become a part of future Christmas celebrations, another tradition.

Baking a cake on Christmas Day is a simple task, yet the symbolism can become the capstone of your holiday experience. Christmas is meant to be joyous. It is also a reminder to share the light that came to earth on that night long ago.

Put the spotlight back on Christ, and your Christmas will be one that springs you and your loved ones into the New Year focused on the real meaning of the season.

Happy baking and mighty Christmas!

~~~~~~~~

A Shortcut to the Spirit of the Season

Need help finding a child to sponsor? In a web search, type in "child sponsorship" and review the links. Look for a group that will assign a specific child, provide you with updates, and allow you to exchange letters with your child.

A Bonus Day

Filling a Big Box

The day after Christmas is one of the busiest days of the year at many stores. It is when millions line up to exchange gifts for either refunds or something else they want. Odds are, you probably have a number of gifts you don't need. Yet before you trade them in, maybe it's time to see if what you don't want might be something someone else could use. By giving to others on the day after the holiday, you are making a huge Christmas statement. In other words, the giving season doesn't have to be over just yet.

Most Americans don't realize that in every English-speaking country except our own, the day after Christmas is one of the biggest days of the year for giving. Called Boxing Day, it's a holiday tradition that for centuries has greatly enhanced the lives of many of the world's poorest people.

With roots tied to charity that began in churches, this special day is one that each of us ought to adopt and make into a holiday tradition.

Boxing Day was the first recognized holiday that fully incorporated Christ's teachings to reach out to the poor. In fact, that was its sole purpose. Boxing Day was established to encourage those who had much to share their blessings in order to minister to those who had little or nothing.

The beginnings of Boxing Day go back centuries to the Middle Ages. During that time, in churches throughout England, money boxes were placed near the buildings' entrances. All year long, on top of their normal gifts to the church, parishioners were asked to place extra alms in the box to honor the memory of the apostle Stephen. On December 26, at the Feast of St. Stephen, these boxes were opened by church leaders. The contents were then distributed to the poorest of the poor.

Over time, the custom was expanded beyond the church doors. Soon household servants began to find boxes filled with food, clothing, and money on the day after Christmas. This practice became the way for the master to say thank you to those who had served on the estate all year long. Eventually this custom of the wealthy was expanded to include gifts for bakers, blacksmiths, newspaper boys, butchers, and everyone else who provided services for the masters' households.

In the middle of the 1800s, with Queen Victoria and her

husband Prince Albert leading the way, Boxing Day was pushed back to its roots. The queen asked people of substance to not only give rewards to those who served their households but also share gifts with the poor. These gifts of food, clothing, and household goods were usually carried in trunks or boxes, and the day was soon officially called Boxing Day.

Today Boxing Day is celebrated in Great Britain as well as in Canada, Australia, New Zealand, and even parts of China. The holiday exists solely to recognize society's need to reach out to those who are not as fortunate. It is not about tithing; it's about going that extra mile and sharing blessings beyond the normal ten percent given.

In Luke 14:13 Jesus said, "When you give a banquet, invite the poor, the crippled, the lame, the blind." For the past few days, most of us have enjoyed banquets, but have we included those our Lord asked us to invite? Probably not. Our Christmas was for family. But on Boxing Day we can live out those words found in Luke.

The first step might be to share a bit of the bounty of our Christmas harvest. Look through your gifts to see if you can spot some things a charity or a poor family could use. Instead of fighting the return lines at the stores, consider giving away those items, in keeping with the full spirit of Christmas. This simple act puts the spotlight back on Christ and gives you a chance to live out the command implied in

Luke 12:48: "To whom much is given ... much will be required" (NKJV).

Find a box, fill it with the extras you don't need, and seek out those who could benefit from having you share your blessings. The poor might not have been invited to your feast, but it's not too late to make them feel that you and the Lord have not forgotten them during the holiday season. Begin a new tradition in your family with your generosity. Invite friends to join you. Spread the word. Eventually Boxing Day could become an important holiday in America too.

~~~~~~~~~~

A Shortcut to the Spirit of the Season

Don't let unneeded gifts sit in a closet. Find a needy person through a local church, the Salvation Army, the United Way, or even your local school. Give a gift to help those in need.

Stories behind Christmas Boxed Set

Ace Collins,
Bestselling Author

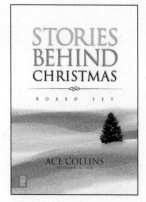

Since angels sang when Jesus was born, music has been as much a part of Christmas as candy canes, Christmas trees, and other beloved traditions of the season. Now you and your family can deepen your celebration of Christ's birth as you learn the stories and spiritual significance of our most cherished holiday songs and traditions.

Do you understand the meaning of "God Rest Ye Merry Gentlemen"? Why do we use red and green at Christmas? What is the origin of the Christmas tree? Do you know the unusual history behind "O Holy Night"?

Written by popular music historian and bestselling author Ace Collins, the three books in this beautiful boxed set unlock the origins and meanings of best-loved carols, hymns, and songs. They also explain traditions as familiar yet little understood as mistletoe, ornaments, stockings, and holly. From the cloisters of fifth-century monks, to the frontlines of World War II, to Hollywood sets and Nashville recording studios, Collins takes you on a journey that will warm your heart and enrich your experience of this brightest of holiday seasons.

Softcover Set: 978-0-310-28112-2

Farraday Road

Ace Collins,
Bestselling Author

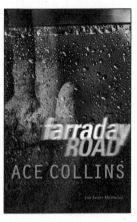

A quiet evening ends in murder on a muddy mountain road.

Local attorney Lije Evans and his beautiful wife, Kaitlyn, are gunned down. But the killers don't expect one of their victims to live. After burying Kaitlyn, Lije is on a mission to find her killer — and solve a mystery that has more twists and turns than an Ozark-mountain back road.

When the trail of evidence goes cold, complicated by the disappearance of the deputy who found Kaitlyn's body at the scene of the crime, Lije is driven to find out why he and his wife were hunted down and left for dead along Farraday Road. He begins his dangerous investigation with no clues and little help from the police. As he struggles to uncover evidence, will he learn the truth before the killers strike again?

Softcover: 978-0-310-27952-5

Pick up a copy today at your favorite bookstore!

ZONDERVAN®
.com